Loose Threads

Loose Threads

STORIES TO KEEP
QUILTERS IN STITCHES

HELEN KELLEY

Voyageur Press

First published in 2008 by Voyageur Press, an imprint of MBI Publishing Company, 400 First Avenue North, Suite 300, Minneapolis, MN 55401 USA

Voyageur Press titles are also available at discounts in bulk quantity for industrial or sales-promotional use. For details write to Special Sales Manager at MBI Publishing Company, 400 First Avenue North, Suite 300, Minneapolis, MN 55401 USA.

To find out more about our books, join us online at www.voyageurpress.com.

ISBN-13: 978-0-7603-3203-0

Editor: Margret Aldrich
Designer: Jennie Maass
On the cover: "Wednesday Keeps Us in Stitches" © Sandi Wickersham, detail

Printed in the United States of America

Library of Congress Cataloging-in-Publication Data

Kelley, Helen, 1927–
 Loose threads : stories to keep quilters in stitches / Helen Kelley.
 p. cm.
 ISBN 978-0-7603-3203-0 (plc w/ jkt)
 1. Quilting–United States–Miscellanea. 2. Patchwork–United States–Miscellanea. 3. Quilts–United States–Miscellanea. I. Title.
TT835.K46155 2008
746.46'0973--dc22
 2008000359

Dedication

Some bits of fluff tied together with a few loose threads, dedicated especially to you from me. HLK

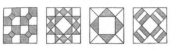

CONTENTS

Preface

I remember the incident very clearly. I was hunched over the copy machine in the office supplies store, concentrating, playing with designs for a twelve-inch friendship quilt block. I enlarged shapes, cut them out and rearranged them. Suddenly, I was aware of a hand moving softly across my back. The hand wandered. It stroked; it plucked. I spun around to face the woman standing behind me.

"What are you doing?" I asked, bewildered.

She was embarrassed.

"Oh," she said, "I was just picking the loose threads off of the back of your shirt."

Later, thinking about those loose threads, I realized how much a part of me they are. Those loose threads are always with me, following me everywhere. They are the little bits and pieces of things that litter my clothes and my life. They are the shreds of every day things and parts of all that happen to me. I am a hand-quilter and in the hours I spend at my quilt frame, I work quietly, stitching inch by inch. While I am stitching, my mind plays games. It looks back over the moments of each day, wandering and wondering. These mental meanderings are my loose threads. They are thoughts about the people around me. They are about daily comings and goings. They are about pattern possibilities and color choices. Because I am lucky enough to love this quilting that I do, these loose threads fill my thoughts with joy and curiosity and laughter, and I write them down.

Sometimes I write about my family. In earlier times it seemed as if I worked overtime to keep the five children fed, washed, ironed, mended, and healthy. Now they are all grown up and gone away, but thanks to the miracle of cell phones, I hear from them regularly so that I can follow their lives. As I sit and stitch, I sort out the length and breadth of their activities. The grandchildren and great-grandchildren seem to have come along in steady succession and because I have vowed to make a really unique quilt for each of them, some of my thoughts are about inventing new ways to capture their special memories in fabric. This bevy of people—my children, grandchildren, and "greats"—inspire me with their surprising energy and creative productivity. However, the very best thing in my life is my husband, Bill, who encourages me to write down my musings as they flutter through my head. *Quilters Newsletter* began printing these rambling thoughts years ago in their magazine. These good friends were the first to dub them "Loose Threads."

Sometimes my loose threads are about the absurdities that I find lurking in my regular routine. I know that I have a quirky sense of humor, and stuck doors, spilled breakfast cereal, and trips to the fabric store often strike me as very funny. Our lives, yours and mine, are a tapestry of minor moments and I have learned to look at them, laugh at them, and love them. For instance, we have a congregation of squirrels that gather in our yard to cavort and chatter in our walnut trees. As I stand in my workroom early in the morning drinking my first cup of coffee, I watch them from my window. One squirrel has made himself a shallow basin in the dirt beneath the forsythia bush. He is a strange creature, probably mad, because as I watch, he somersaults gleefully in this grassy pit that he has made. I watch his little bottom and his feet fly up and over his ears. Around and around he tumbles. He is exuberant. What ridiculous exhilaration! I relate to that joy because it is so much like the unfettered pleasure I experience when I am feeling fabric, letting it slide through my fingers, watching it change colors in the clear light and discovering grand new ways to stitch it together into fanciful gardens or geometric puzzles. My

- - - - -
13

mind does joyful gymnastics, too, and when I write it about it, it becomes a Loose Threads essay.

Sometimes, my thoughts are spun from my friendships. Quilters are interesting people, and I am grateful to them for enriching my life. I write about them, and when I put it down on paper, it too becomes a Loose Thread.

Sometimes there are brief moments in all of our lives, flashes of discovery and wonder. Finding a rainbow in the sky is a moment of illumination, seeing the colors playing against the depth of the deep purple on one side and blazing with sunshine on the other. All that translucent color has such potential. Marveling at it, I make a trip to the fabric store where I play with reds and purples and yellows to make my own rainbow. The awe I feel as I watch a rolling wave, a darting bird, or the breathless silence of a sunset makes me pause to marvel about miracles. These thoughts spin about in my head and I write about them. They become Loose Threads.

The evening news, a snarled sewing machine, and the local quilt show are all cob-webby notions and mental bits of floss. They are the fiber of my life and I weave them into stories. The wonder of it is that I am an ordinary person, a typical quilter. The fabric of my days is much the same as yours; you and I have so much in common. We share the frantic activity of daily challenges and quiet triumphs. Whether you are a quilter or an appreciator, a lover of beautiful things, you know exactly what I mean, and so I have written down these Loose Threads especially for you.

Chapter 1

EVERY STITCH
TELLS A STORY

Thoughts on Masterpieces

Let's get one thing straight right from the beginning . . . I am not what my mother used to call a "spring chicken." On the other hand, I am not a fossil, either. One recent Sunday night, we watched *Masterpiece Theatre*. We sat in the living room with our feet propped up comfortably and our coffee cups in our hands. The movie was a good one, filled with the emotional ups and downs that we would rather be spectators to than experience ourselves. When it was over, a commentator chatted with the audience, discussing the story and its background.

"This is a charming period piece set in 1946," he said.

"Whoa," I shouted. "What did you call it?"

He proceeded to point out that the costumes were well designed, quite appropriate for the time. I could have pointed out to him that I probably still have some of those quaint costumes in a closet somewhere. The young ingénue could have been me, and I am not a character from a period piece.

It's true that I have gray hair, and a few wrinkles in my face, but I make quilts with pretty good eyesight and lots of enthusiasm. I move with a spring in my step. I relish untangling puzzles, and the problems of design. I enjoy pizza on Sunday nights, walking through the grass in my bare feet, meeting new friends and seeing new places, reading exciting books, and listening to emotional, cymbal-crashing music. I am not an antique.

Somewhere in the recent past, the word "antique" has been updated. Antique used to mean anything more than one hundred years old. Then, we began seeing signs in shops that advertised "Antiques and Collectibles." Anything that was older than the span of a teenager's mind became an "Antique." I am still surprised when I go into a store where I see "Antique Quilts" advertised and find a vast array of Grandmother's Flower Garden quilts in the lovely sherbet colors of the 1920s and 1930s. Those quilts are not one hundred years old. Not yet, anyway!

Let's look at the semantics of the word antique. My thesaurus describes an antique as "a relic." It also mentions words like "ancient, moth-eaten, old-fashioned and timeworn." Some Grandmother's Flower Garden quilts might qualify by this definition, but most of those old quilts are charming; they capture our memories and our affections. By the true meaning of the word, though, they are not honest-to-goodness antiques.

Looking at the past from our modern perspective, we view old wars, houses, politics, child-rearing methods, recipes, transportation and, yes, quilts as quaint. We've adapted the term "antique" because it wraps quilts in the warm glow of our recollection. We have a love affair with the past. We chuckle over pleats and puckers in old work and think of them as charming, We classify naive, roughly-made quilts in the category of fine folk art. We try to recapture the warm patina of the old apron design fabrics from the early twentieth-century quilts in our own reproduction, contemporary quilts. Actually, whether the older quilts are antiques by the original definition is no longer important, because, quite simply, they charm us. "Old" is an affectionate term.

Quilters and quiltmakers do not, however, fall into the same category. Antique quilts may stir our affections, but remember this—as a venerable quilter, unlike an old quilt, I am neither "cute" nor "quaint." Like me, many of you were quilters in the twentieth century. Now that we live in the twenty-first century, you have become a veteran quilter. When the younger people of today remember back to the twentieth century, they will think of it as the Dark Ages and you, my friend may very well find yourself portrayed as a character in a "period piece." Instead, I prefer to think of all of us and our quilts as "Masterpieces."

Life on an Ocean Wave

My morning routine is a ritual, a ceremony—rather like breaking a bottle of champagne across the bow of a ship when it is christened. It is how I launch myself into each day's new adventure.

I stand in the kitchen feeling the warmth of a mug of coffee in my hand and breathe in the tantalizing smell. When I'm refreshed and alert, I am ready to firm up my plans for a new quilt. The vision of this quilt may be one that I have carried around in my head for months, but now is the time to make it a reality. Setting off on a new challenge is an exciting experience, but with each beginning there are some hard decisions to be made.

I start by making a rough sketch on a tablet of paper. From there I go on to drafting the blocks. Once I have figured out the geometries of my pieced stars or Flying Geese, I move on to sketching the shapes for my leafy applique trees that will cover the calico hills or the flowers to make a sumptuous bouquet. When these units are drawn, I make duplicates on my copy machine and cut them out to play with. That part's not so hard.

Strangely, though, a big challenge comes when I tack a large piece of paper on my wall that is the size my new quilt will be.

I need to divide the space into areas for patchwork blocks and applique fields, but I am becalmed and adrift. The thought of "where" and "how" to begin is overwhelming. The idea of making that first pencil stroke on that flawless paper takes the wind out of my sails.

For me, the solution is to close my eyes, hold my breath, and strike out blindly with my pencil to make the first firm, black mark somewhere—anywhere—on that blank paper. Having taken away the perfection of that great, white space makes it feel comfortable. Now I can begin. I can play with those cutouts, moving them around on the paper until the design pleases me. All those ideas that were floating around in my head can be fixed firmly in place on the paper.

When I am ready to begin cutting and sewing, I face another difficult moment: cutting into my length of expensive fabric. I am acutely aware of the days and the miles invested in the hunt for this exactly right yardage. It is beautiful; it is immaculate; it is costly; and it is irreplaceable because it was the last of its kind on the bolt. The solution, I have discovered, is to make a first, nonthreatening cut by neatly removing the selvedge of the material, a cut of little consequence. Having made that first slice, I am freed. The fabric is no longer untouchable. It has become friendly.

I do not think of myself as a timid person, but beginning anything new takes a certain amount of grace and a certain amount of grit. Anything that one cares deeply about doing is usually scary. Once I have worked out my dream and drawn the shapes on paper and begun cutting into my lovely fabric, I am prepared. My course is charted, and I am ready to cruise.

I listen to good music as I cut my fabric pieces and play with the shapes and colors. Making this quilt becomes fun, just as it should be. My confidence is renewed, and I feel clever and capable. It took courage to begin, but now that I have gotten my sea legs, I foresee smooth sailing. My moment of quiet reflection over a mug of coffee at the beginning of the day started the day's journey. It firmed my resolution and focused me. It launched me and I sailed out onto a pleasant sea.

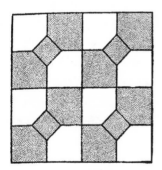 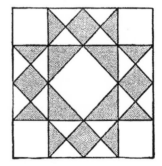

Mama, Where Did I Come From?

Did a Good Fairy hide me under a cabbage leaf? Did I spring, like Aphrodite, from a seashell? Was I left behind after an alien visit? Did I arrive safely cradled in a doctor's black bag? Certainly, it is not possible that I could ever have descended, like many Americans and much of the world, from pioneer stock. I am not rugged and forbearing.

I watch in amazement when cavorting children leap, laughing, from docks or rocks to swim in icy waters. Cold water appalls me.

On TV shows, we see people coming down from Mt. Everest exhilarated from the challenge of conquering great rocks and enormous heights. Dashing my body against craggy landscapes is not my idea of fun. Marathon runners propel themselves along exhausting racecourses, running and testing themselves and their endurance. There seems to be a large part of the world that is invigorated by the challenge of a survival experience.

I love warm water and central heating and carpeted floors under my bare feet. My car is equipped with air-conditioning and heat control and comfortable seats. My workroom has electric lights that flick on with a switch and turn my nighttime surroundings into a world of brilliant sunlight. For all of these things, I am grateful. All of these things I cherish.

Bill recently dropped a magazine into my lap. "I thought you might be interested in this," he said. He pointed to a review of a book, a discussion of the myth about the pleasures of early American domesticity, the laughter of frontier social gatherings, and the delights of being courted by rough-and-ready pioneer men. Lovely stories have been woven around those times when women survived cold water, candlelight, and a life of sickness, with meager food, a lack of fuel, and body-bruising work.

The review discussed the process of indigo dyeing. Indigo, itself, had a putrid odor, and the procedure of producing blue cloth in vats of salvaged urine was not a pleasant one. Yet, women did it. The article pointed out that our foremothers endured these hardships, but what it failed to recognize was the miracle of it all. Women fed their families, protected them, clothed them, and kept them warm in spite of the fact that life was often a lonely, frightening, exhausting, and unpleasant experience. They still managed to nurture a germ of beauty in their hearts. Their quilts show us that. Some of them were simple squares of fabrics salvaged from salesmen's sample books or scraps from worn-out clothing that were hastily stitched together and tied with string or yarn. Fast bedding was a necessity when winters closed in rapidly. Yet, consider the other quilts, the glorious ones that have come down to us, also from those quiltmakers. The nonquilting world often fails to understand what you and I know well, that quilts don't "just happen." Beautiful quilts take time. They take vision. They take perseverance.

So, I am in awe of those earlier women. They made wonderful quilts, and the creating of those beautiful quilts may have been the thread that held their minds and hearts together through times of bleakness. I understand this, and so I wonder if we all don't have that same gene in our makeup. We no longer have to sew by kerosene lantern. We no longer have to find our way to the privy in the dark of bitter-cold nights; We no longer have to bar the door against bears or exist on smoked meats and tough, dry bread. Still, when we sit down to make a quilt, we face the same basic challenges that those women did. We make fabric choices, we cut them into pieces, and we sew the pieces together to create a tangible testament of the vision in our hearts.

I think that it does not matter how I got "here." The important thing is that I carry in my heart that enduring love of making quilts. The remarkable thing is that I am here now, in this time, making quilts in contemporary comfort with current fabric and tools, and that I have the leisure time to do it. The wonder of it is that I still have, just as those earlier women did, quilt visions in my head.

I Am a Lady

Some years ago in a lecture in California, Sandi Fox told about a quilt in which she discovered the quilted message, "I am a lady."

I was reminded of that quilt the other day when an English friend commented that she could always tell if a woman was a lady if her draperies were lined. That would make me only half a lady since the draperies in the living room are lined, but my workroom draperies hang naked.

My mother used to say that a lady always wore a slip and never, never used perfume before noon. All of that sounds old-fashioned, I suppose. And yet young people of today have their standards, too. Only now they don't call it being a "lady." What do they call it? "Cool"? Or currently is it being "hot"? Whatever is today's jargon to describe ladylike behavior? I find it difficult to keep up with what's "in" and what's "out," much less what kind of behavior is considered ladylike now. I do know that last night when I was at the Science Museum, a girl came in that door over beside the giant iguana and she had on a skirt that was so short it would have scandalized our mothers and grandmothers. Everyone turned to admire that stunning, shapely young lady in her miniskirt for she was certainly acceptable.

- - - - -

I wonder, what makes an acceptable, well-mannered quilt? Is it a matter of wearing the proper colors? Must its thread be clipped neatly, its fabric unrumpled and well-fitting? Must it behave nicely, acting in a temperate manner—not too loudly, but daintily, attractively?

I have a well-mannered friend who is always a lady. She is kind. She thinks before she speaks, never saying anything unseemly or in an inappropriate manner. She is never awkward. Everyone loves her. She never hurts feelings, is never rude.

I do believe that beneath her placid exterior, I shock her on occasion. I tend to laugh heartily. I say things that I think are hysterically funny. Sometimes they are; sometimes they aren't. Sometimes I go to the grocery store in my purple jogging suit. My friend always wears an attractive skirt and stockings. Sometimes I arrive at meetings late—panting and disheveled. My friend is always on time and neat. There is no doubt about it: She is a lady. What, in heaven's name, am I?

And, too, there is a question about quilt behavior. Some quilts are obviously well-mannered. Some are pristine, all-white, feathered, and stippled. Certainly these are ladies. Some quilts are trimmed with proper chintz, some gently embroidered, some delicately embellished with laces, some sweetly color harmonized— all with their fabrics clean and neat, their lumps and bumps controlled. They are all ladies.

- - - - -

And I've seen quilts with raucous colors, quilts that swirled and frothed, quilts that did all sorts of unexpected things and, by golly, they were ladies, too.

Sweets for the Sweet

My mother was a fabulous cook. When I was growing up, dinner guests who came to our house invariably brought her a sampler box of candy. You know the kind I mean, don't you? The boxes are like treasure chests and are printed with a design that looks like cross-stitched flowers on linen. When we opened that box, each sweet square and round dollop and little pillow with chocolatey squiggles and flourishes on it was cradled in a ruffled paper cup. Some of the most delectable pieces were wrapped in golden foil.

There was a chart on the inside of the lid that told us exactly where to find the maple creams and the butter pecans, the almond pastes and the orange fondants. Allowed to have "just one piece," we children studied that chart carefully. Our mouths watered, and the privilege of choosing one piece—any one of them—was a child's dream.

Now that I am all grown up, the joy of sampling is still a privilege I cherish. My imagining, my pleasuring, and the final choosing isn't as much about my taste buds now as it is about ideas that make my fingers itch. Now, all of the intriguing, delicious things that I like to "taste" and "test" are in quilt shows or are pictured in my latest quilt magazine. There, wonderful delights are laid out for me like a banquet. They tempt me, and I am no longer restricted to "just one."

Some choices are big projects and amazing challenges, as anyone who has ever undertaken to applique an entire Hawaiian quilt top can tell you. Projects of that sort are designed for quilters who have enormous reserves of energy and astonishing skills. Hooray for them! Others just starting out on their quilting adventure might prefer to make smaller pieces in their quiet times. Some quilters love traditional pieced blocks and graceful borders; others love devising unusual techniques with exotic fabrics. The amazing thing about this treasure chest of quilting patterns and techniques and styles is that we can pick and choose and savor just like I sampled the nougats and the syrupy fruits in that box of candy.

New quilters developing their skills sometimes find their eyes are bigger than their stomachs. If they undertake a challenge that is too far beyond their experience, they can lose heart. But everyone needs options, exciting things we can do at our own pace.

My tastes developed as I nibbled at new things. In the beginning—just like all newbies—I learned to thread a needle from a patient teacher. I moved ahead, learning step by step. As a child my very first stitches were taken on dishtowels and pot holders. Those beginning stitches were not a pretty sight, but they prepared me to make better stitches as I moved along to quilts. Each project on the way taught me something. I've dabbled in so many things. Some of the things that I tasted, I loved. Some of them were less exciting, some disappointing. Some of them were disasters. And some of them exhilarated me. Over time I learned what colors make my heart sing, what kind of batting works best for me, and what techniques and designs make me happiest.

If you are a quilter who wrestles with the strain of your job or if you are short on energy and time because you are raising a rambunctious family, you need smaller, easier challenges. That's okay. Quilting should be therapy for the over-burdened, not a chore done in spite of life's pressures.

The variety of delights in our quilter's sampler box gives us choices, for both the quilters who prefer the simple pleasures of relaxed quilting and the ultra-ambitious, amazing achievers. We should be able to dip into our sampler chest and taste and enjoy. I love caramels and the gooey sweetness that melts in my mouth. I love the pleasure of hand applique, too. What sorts of things are your favorites? Paper piecing, rotary cutting, or playing with colors? You and I have choices, every one of us. There are wonderful hidden treasures in our quilting sampler box. Every time we open it up, there is the possibility of a new adventure.

I can open a box of candy and pick my favorite flavor, but the sweetest pleasure of all is surely the joy I find when I sample from all my quilting possibilities.

- - - - -

Doing What Comes Naturally

After grabbing a few essentials from the aisles at the grocery store the other night, I fell in line behind other people at the cash register. An attractive woman was in front of me, methodically moving her groceries from her basket onto the conveyor belt. Her son stood behind her, a nicely dressed boy, about sixth-grade age, quiet, and well behaved. But then an almost invisible flicker moved through the boy's body. Then another. He shifted his weight a bit, and slowly raised his arm. With his wrist bent at an acute angle, his left shoulder projected forward. Abruptly, his head turned to the left as his body followed the direction of his thrusting hand. As if by magic, the young man transformed into a break-dancer. He gyrated rhythmically behind his mother as she continued to unload her cart. He moved silently, gliding hypnotically in his astonishing dance to soundless music. His angular, fluid motions were amazing to watch, not only because he was so talented, but because it was all happening in such a preposterous place.

Later, when I told the story to a friend, she smiled. "Well, I suppose the lesson here is, if it feels good, do it." It was a simple, profound thought, and at that moment, listening to the wisdom of it, I found peace with myself.

- - - - -

For years I've felt uncertain about the quilts that I make. I love looking at contemporary quilts, those with the elaborate machine embroidery and soft, raw-edged appliqué—wildly innovative quilts with imaginative embellishments, daring colors, and bold geometrics. I've told myself that I must keep up with the times, becoming free and spontaneous, comfortable with loose edges and raw trimmings, with overlapping fabrics held in place by an assortment of glue and machine stitchings, making arty quilts sewn together with miracle machine quilting. But this picture of a quiltmaker doesn't seem to match my style. My results with this kind of quilting seem awkward and pretentious.

I also love traditional quilts. They are so satisfying with their comfortable colors. I am drawn to both appliqued blocks and to those pieced in clever, subtle repeats creating rainbow kaleidoscopes. Quilts stitched around and around with feathered borders dazzle me. My finished quilts never look like the antique masterpieces I so admire. When I plan a quilt, I begin with those graceful, old-fashioned patterns that speak to me. Somewhere in the process of making that quilt, those patterns turn renegade. They have minds of their own. By the time I've finished with the quilt, I've wandered from those familiar traditions and travelled in unexpected directions.

Therefore, not being successful at either contemporary experimentation or sweet, old-style

- - - - -

quilting, I make my quilts in the way that little voice inside me tells me to do. Over the years, I've apologized for my less-sophisticated quilts. I have explained my lapses and inadequacies to those who have spent their lives creating traditional quilts from zillions of pieces of gentle-colored fabrics stitched together with elegance.

Now I understand myself. My quilts are hand quilted because quilting on my machine feels awkward to me. My quilts are made, usually, from fabrics purchased straight off the bolt because I enjoy the challenge of devising visual effects with printed fabrics from my favorite quilt store. Dying fabric is an occupation in itself, and time spent coloring fabric in lovely tints and glowing shades is time I would rather spend in other ways. I admire cleverly painted embellishments, lightning zigzags of rough appliqued edges, and transparencies created with layers of unique fabrics, but I've discovered that turning under the edges of my applique patches smoothly and evenly gives me enormous pleasure. I know myself well enough now to know that I work in careful, calculated steps with tried-and-true techniques. It is quite impossible for me to relax and let wonderful things simply happen. My loose edges must be tacked down. My ravels and ripples must be disciplined. I can look at those miraculous pieces that other people have made and marvel at them, but they are not part of who I am.

That dancing boy who twirled and swooped and glided in the grocery store taught me a lesson, and I am grateful. I do what I do because it feels good; I can be proud of that. I make my quilts in my own way, because it just comes naturally.

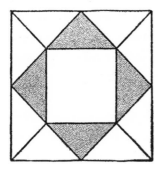 

Getting Down to the Nitty-Gritty

In the year 79 A.D., Mt. Vesuvius exploded. It blew smoke high into the air. Hot cinders and wet ashes poured from its top, spilling down its sides, filling the valley below like sand in a bucket. Life stopped in the city of Pompeii at that moment. Nearly two thousand years later, archeological excavations uncovered what life had been like in that geological time capsule.

The scientists discovered that Pompeii had farms with stables and barns and vineyards and gardens. Families enjoyed mirrors and dishes. The cleaner citizens took baths in tubs similar to the ones in our own bathrooms. Perfume containers, wine vessels, oil lamps, and cloth were discovered. Politicians may not have been much different then, for election slogans decorated the walls of houses. A baker transporting loaves of bread left his mark in the ashes. When Pompeiian civilization was uncovered, a portrait of each person as he or she lived at that moment in history was exposed.

I got to thinking today, what would historians deduce if, at this moment, all my workroom would be covered with ashes and silt and dug out in two thousand years? There in the middle of the floor lies my large pot lid, good for making perfect circles, better even than the chalk and string. The fabric in my closet is piled high, so high, in fact, that if an earthquake accompanied the eruption, the fabric would fall over and bury me. Piled about me are my pliers (for pulling stubborn needles through thick fabrics), and soap slivers for marking dark fabrics. There are my favorite stout toenail scissors for cutting applique templates without shaggy, little points, and sandpaper to hold my fabric as I mark it. In a jar are knitting needles for poking things, and lamps, lamps, lamps. There are three wastebaskets (count 'em), books, books, and more books, and cardboard boxes stacked one on top of another in the corners. Over all of this are pins scattered in a glittering, decorative effect.

Two thousand years from now, if an archeologist happened to sift through ashes and soot and dig down to my workroom, would she be able to draw any conclusions about me, about my work? How would this person in her futuristic silver suit and boots decide I had spent my daily life? Would this scientist discover my pot lid and believe I had been a cook? Would the sandpaper and pliers indicate I had been a carpenter? Would she determine that I had been literate with all those shelves of books? All those soap slivers would surely prove to her that I was clean.

Would this probing, keen-witted archeologist put together all of the clues and conclude that I had been a quilter? Or most obvious of all, would an announcement be flashed across the galaxy from satellite to satellite announcing to the universe that she had found the home of a junk dealer?

- - - - -

The Ten Steps of Separation from My Fabric

I have just filled the trunk of my car with fabric. I have filled up the back seat, too, and I have filled the passenger seat. This I have done because I have cleaned out my stash. It had grown to monstrous proportions. The situation had happened gradually over a period of many years and it is one that happens to every quilter eventually.

A quilter's stash is a deeply personal thing and to help you through this difficult period in your own life when it happens to you, I thought it might help you if I wrote down my Ten Steps of Separation from my Fabric.

1. The Avoidance Factor: I needed a special shade of blue for the quilt that I am currently making and I stood for some time in front of my fabric cupboard gathering courage to plunge into it, to wallow into the heaps of closely packed, wadded, jammed fabrics. Instead, I went to the fabric store to see the blues neatly arranged in beautifully lighted color-displays.

2. The Organizational Challenge: Long ago, my plan was to fill my eight shelves with six piles of fabric in rainbow colors and one pile of white and one of black. It seemed

so simple, but my piles cross-bred and mutated and sprouted cars and mountains and elephants and stars and American flags, and nothing made sense any more.

3. Access and Scrutiny: Prowling through my fabrics turned into a kind of excavation process and less like an artistic endeavor in which I discovered amazing things like pieces that had fallen behind drawers or been stuffed into empty spaces.

4. A Historical Review: Laying my fabrics out on the floor before me, I realized that I had been saving material for sixty or seventy years, hand-dyes, batiks, 1930s pastels, bold geometric prints from the 1940s, and Bicentennial prints from the 1970s. Somebody else can love these or leave 'em. Out they go!

5. Reality Value: There are old pieces of shirts and skirts with holes cut into them. Somehow I never threw anything away; I should have.

6. The Chaos Theory: This theory probes the idea that there is actually an underlying order in what seems to be universal disorder. There may be a masterpiece quilt lurking in the chaotic, murky disorder of my fabric stash, but I will never in this lifetime have the stamina to discover its hidden essence lurking there.

- - - - -

7. Spatial Considerations: The simple fact is that there was "no more room in the inn."

8. An Issue of Morality: This fabric represents an embarrassment of riches and the question is "Should anybody on God's green earth have this much fabric?"

9. The Security Problem: Getting the door of my fabric cupboard closed again was no longer possible.

10. Environmental Management: At least disposing of my fabric will not litter the landscape. People love fabric. All I have to do is open up my car trunk and I will have quilters lined up with open hands to take away my old fabric and turn it into new quilts. Fabric is good. Friends are good.

— — — —

I have cleared, cleaned and swept my workroom. I am organized. I am ready to begin again.

That Old Time Religion

Right in the middle of supper last night, Bill said, "Let's go to the movies." We put on our coats and off we went to a little old neighborhood movie theater not far from us that has been restored to art deco splendor.

The movie for the evening was *Singing in the Rain*, itself restored to splendor. There we sat, under twinkling chandeliers with the balconies on either side of the stage glowing with hidden lights. The movie screen in front of us was so close that we could see the individual raindrops glistening on the twirling, wet umbrellas in the film, and we were caught up in the glamour. It was magic to see Debbie Reynolds again as she was at 21 years old and to watch Gene Kelly's feet tap so fast they chattered.

Seeing that old movie in its rightful setting was poignant. We were charmed. There was a communal sigh when the movie ended and then enthusiastic clapping. The man behind me said, "I've seen this movie so many times, it's like a religious experience."

"What church do you go to?" I asked.

Maybe that's why I began quilting so many years ago. I am touched by images of old quilts in their rightful settings. Living in this contemporary environment, I am moved by the efforts of quilters from one hundred to two hundred years ago, when they worked in limited space with only candles or kerosene lamps with needles as precious as anything else they owned. Those women did not have fabric heaped on shelves in awesome stashes. Their time was measured by the tick of a mechanical clock, and their moments were not eased by air conditioning and central heating. Everyday chores were energy-consuming, and in that time of fewer conveniences and more challenges, people worked with considerably more effort to stitch their visions into their quilts.

I am awed by the people who produced those old quilted wonders, and when I see them spread out on antique beds with sunlight sifting in on them, it is like a religious experience for me. Those images stir me.

Today our circumstances are much easier. We have the tools and an environment to encourage us. Life is more convenient. If I want another piece of fabric, I get into my car and drive a mile or even ten to a quilt store and search through bolts in every hue. If I lose a needle, guiltlessly I pull another one from the pack. If I want inspiration and help, I turn on my computer or open a magazine.

I look at those amazing medallion quilts from 250 years ago. I see those rusty red stars and gentle pink Irish Chains from 150 years ago. I finger the frayed edges of pastel lambs and Bo Peep prints from 75 years ago, and I am moved.

- - - - -

Tennis Elbow

Years ago, I drove a car that had a really difficult stick shift. It required the muscles of Atlas and the determination of a saint every time I wanted to change gears.

Sometimes manipulating it reduced me to tears, and then one morning I woke to find my right arm swollen and sore. "Tennis elbow" was the diagnosis. I had an abused arm. Such an injury is not a good thing for a quilter, but I found that alternate applications of ice and heat quickly eased the pain and put me back in working order.

This morning I woke with what seems to be "tennis thumb." I have been working hard to finish a small quilt. I have quilted all day, every day for awhile now. My fingers are sore—I had expected them to get that way—but I hadn't expected the pain across my thumb joint. Then I remembered the treatment for my elbow incident, and I began ice and heat applications on my thumb.

Sitting with a bag of frozen vegetables wrapped around my hand gave me time to think. What could I have done differently to avoid this distress? The quilt that I am working on is an intricate reproduction of a Gothic building, a structure that looks like a stone wedding cake. The great windows and doors are surrounded with carved swirls and apostrophes. The balustrade across the eaves is crenellated and adorned with elaborately chiseled indentations. The roof ridge looks like a piece of stone lace. Across the face of the building are more than a dozen statues. The triple towers reach high, piercing the blue sky. Because this is such a large building on such a small quilt, I outline quilted around the edges of the building with only a narrow allowance, one that seems in proportion. It gave me the space to quilt more detail around the ancient elegance. Given another chance to plan my quilting, would I have quilted with a wider allowance? It would have required fewer stitches, but I think not. I like seeing the fine detail blossom and swell on the quilt. We make our choices.

When I originally planned the building, I had fewer scrolls and twists and turns—that would have simplified my work. If I had made it easier though, it would not have been a depiction of that architectural wonder that inspired me. No, I would not have planned my quilt any differently. We make our choices.

Could I have been more patient to save myself from tennis thumb? Could I have allotted my quilting time so that I worked every other day instead and finished the quilt over a longer period of time? No, no, never! I love this quilt. I love what is happening to it. It's exciting to see the depth and the detail emerging under my needle.

I need to work on it now, every day, constantly. I love what I am doing. I have a need to see it finished.

The magic of this quilt is worth every pinprick. It is worth an aching thumb. I would not have done anything differently, and if I were to do it again, I would do it exactly the same way. Today I am wrapping my hand in ice and then warming it with heat, and it feels better moment by moment. I am sitting in my chair looking at my quilt, studying it, and savoring it. Tomorrow, I am going to quilt again.

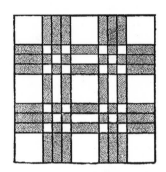
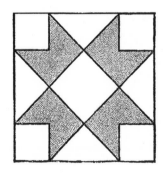
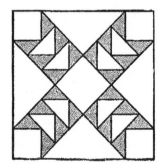

Chapter 2

LICENSE TO QUILT

X-Rated

Every Friday night Bill and I go to dinner at the cafeteria in our local shopping mall. We treat ourselves to rich clam chowder, fried shrimp, and seafood salad slathered in mayonnaise. We help ourselves to slabs of rosy roast beef and salty ham, and we finish with large dishes of ice cream covered with gooey syrup and an assortment of nutty, sugary, sticky confections. In short, we eat everything we want that is bad for our cholesterol, our hearts, our blood pressures and our weights. We have a wonderful time.

When we have finished indulging ourselves, Bill goes to the electronics store to browse, and I wander around the big fabric store to see what's new. We meet in front of the magazine store and leaf through the children's books with their large, colorful drawings of dinosaurs, ogres, and frogs. Last week, I went there to buy a quilt magazine. Some time ago, this shop was a dusty, pulpy place with a shady reputation, but it has upgraded. Now, glossy fashion magazines and hobby publications line the walls.

As I stood at the rear of the store, leafing through quilt magazines on the back shelves, I happened to glance up at the wall and there, directly in front of me, was a door with a little window high up toward the top. I had never noticed that door before. In the center of it was a sign, "For Adults Only."

- - - - -

I don't know why the discovery surprised me so. The management must stock its salacious material behind it. I am sure that door is not new. Obviously, as I gazed at it, I felt as if I were looking at the Gateway to Iniquity, the Portal of Hell. I was, therefore, enormously curious. "I am an adult," I reasoned, "and I can go in there if I want to." I didn't.

It is hard to understand, even at my age, that I am an adult and am allowed to do adult things. I find it surprising that I can stay up late at night, and it remains a source of wonder that nobody can make me eat food that I don't like. I am big enough to drive a car, and I can go alone into the ladies' room in public places. Strangely enough, being adult also means that I can quilt.

Before I was an adult, I didn't know any quilters. I had to teach myself. By the time I figured out the basics, I was old enough, tall enough and, let's hope, smart enough to be an adult.

That was then. Now, kids are lucky. Unlike the days of my childhood, when few of us had mentors to teach us to quilt, many children have mothers and grandmothers who already know how and can teach them. At a tender age, they can get to know the joys of handling fabric and can put together pieces of material to create wonderful mosaics while they are yet young and bright. Children nowadays don't have to wait like I did.

Now that I qualify as an adult, I wear adult-type lingerie, and I am old enough to write checks on my own bank account. I vote on Election Day, and though I learned late, I can quilt. I don't need to push open a mysterious door in the back of the magazine store to enjoy the advantages of being mature. I do not need Parental Guidance. My quilting, you see, is X-rated: Xtremely alluring, Xtravagently self-indulgent, and Xtraordinarily satisfying.

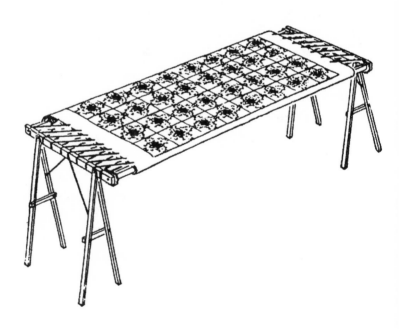

Carpe Diem (Seize the Moment)

I wrote a joke. I printed it on crisp, white paper, and I folded it to tuck into an envelope addressed to America's favorite pocket-sized magazine, the one that prints jokes at the end of every article. I handed a copy to Bill to read. It went this way:

One cold morning, in a quilt shop that was filled with fabrics that were dyed in warm, vibrant colors, I met a man and a woman.

They were browsing through the bolts of green fabrics because she said she wanted to make a wall hanging to match their bathroom.

"Oh," I said, as they fingered tile varieties of soft fabrics, the bold green ones, the swirly ones, "What do you have in your bathroom?"

"My husband," she replied.

Bill looked at me with a blank expression. "It's a joke," I said.

"It's an inside joke," he said. "It's a quilter's joke."

I was astonished. Surely anybody, nor just quilters, could see this joke was very clever. Do quilters have a special sense of humor?

Perhaps they do. Quilters can be very funny people. They laugh at themselves. Their amusement is constant and endless. Their humor filters through into their clever appliqued animals and the unique twists and turns of their pieced quilt patterns. It pervades at bees and at workshops over whirring sewing machines. Quilters see life's odd incidents with an appreciation for the absurdities. Yes, indeed, quilters are very funny people. Quilters would laugh at this joke, I thought.

I began painfully rewriting the joke so that the rest of the world would understand it. When you take a joke apart, examine it word by word and explore its syntax, it is no longer funny. You begin to wonder what you thought was so clever about it in the first place. It loses its spontaneity.

"Ah ha." I thought, "spontaneity." Maybe that is the answer to the question of what makes quilters special. It's their spontaneity, their ability to enjoy life, their impulsive reactions. Quilting often requires the special qualities of improvisation. Quilters have learned quick appreciation and instant response to inspiration.

For instance, right now, I have a quilt top spread out on my floor, and it's pleasant enough. It's a rather mild version of a pieced church, all made in teal blues and browns and greens. The colors are appropriate but bland. The top needs something to make it sing. I've draped embroidery threads of different hues across it, to see if anything might put a spark into it. Suddenly, a rusty brown thread with a tinge of orangey-red shot a flare of light across the quilt top like striking a piece of flint in a tinder box. If I use this to put a tiny embroidered cross on the church roof, it will make music on my quilt. In that momentary flash, that instant of appreciation, I knew spontaneously what to do.

Quilters have learned to be open to the moment. They react impulsively. They respect their intuition and listen to it. Quilters are at their very best when they are excited and when they are inspired—that is, when they are spontaneous. Quilters do, indeed, have a special quality. Their quick ingenuity is related to their funny bones and that's why they can laugh at a good joke.

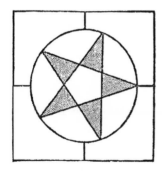
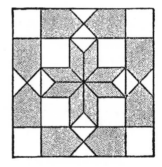

Here's a Toast to Quilting!

I wish I were a psychologist. Perhaps I could then understand the strange phenomenon I have just discovered. I have always thought that my quilters' spread was caused by long hours spent sitting without exercise at my quilt frame. Most certainly the softness around my waist and the undulation of my hips when I walk seem to be caused by lack of deep-knee-bending, waist-twisting and toe-touching, to much eye-squinting and shoulder-hunching. This morning I realized something different.

All this week I have been frantically writing letters, running errands, and being very busy. This morning, instead, I awoke and vacuumed up the stray threads that littered the floor. I watered the plants and put some laundry into the washing machine. Since then, I have been sitting quietly quilting.

For breakfast I usually have a cup of coffee. Then perhaps I have another one and another. Somewhere in between I may have one slice of toast, lightly buttered. It is always adequate. I am busy enough that I don't stop to think of eating until lunch, which may consist of a cup of soup and half a tomato sandwich. I'm not a big eater.

This morning I had my cup of coffee. As the washing machine churned, I sat down to spend the rest of the day stitching on my newest project—and here I am. The pattern is all traced out and I am well-situated with good light. My thread and scissors are close at hand. The breeze coming in the back window is pleasant. There is good music on the radio. And all I can think about is food.

I had hardly taken two stitches when my stomach growled. Since then, it has carried on with increasing commotion. I have thought about potato chips, lovely salted potato chips. Perhaps a Coke, a good stiff one with lots of dark fizz. Pecan cookies! Buttery, and of course rich. A few more stitches and cheese and crackers come to mind.

Now that I look back on my quilting times, I realize that I have spent a lot of it walking back and forth between the quilt frame and kitchen. I set goals by promising myself that when I finish this border strip, I will have a piece of toast spread thick with strawberry jam. When I am finished with that feather, perhaps another piece of toast, this time with peanut butter. The curse of my life, it appears, is the microwave (instant coffee) and that toaster. I have to go back to my quilting now, and all I can think about is apple butter.

It's not the threading that's causing my spreading. It's not the sitting that's unfitting. It's the eating that's defeating.

I Got Music

The stereo speaker sits right beside my quilt frame. I have quilted to music since the beginning of my memory. First, I listened to thick, waxy 78-rpm "platters." I had "Chattanooga Choochoo" and "String of Pearls" and the moaning low trumpet of Clyde McCoy playing "Sugar Blues."

The first year after we were married, LP players came onto the market. We had no washer, no dryer, no vacuum cleaner, and no carpet, but we bought an LP player. That new machine seemed like a miracle. In contrast to the heavy wax records, the LP records were slim and flexible, and because it wasn't necessary to lift the scratchy needle and change the record every three minutes, we were freed from mechanical demands. As I stitched, I listened, and frequently, I leapt up from my sewing and swirled around our apartment to the vibrating strings of golden violins gushing out Viennese waltzes.

The age of the tape recorder was less idyllic. Many of the memories of those years involve twirling the eraser end of a pencil in the little holes of the cassettes, untangling sinuous tape that refused to perform neatly and precisely. Those years wound their way through an array of Pete Seeger; Peter, Paul and Mary; and rollicking folk music.

Now, we have a CD player. It is heavenly. Music has always had a heavenly quality. In Renaissance art, painted angels with flowing hair and diaphanous robes blow trumpets and strum lutes. It is interesting to note that I have never seen a Renaissance angel holding a needle and a quilting hoop. I am sure that this was the choice of the artists and not necessarily that of the angels. After all, quilts are inspired creations, too. Quilts and music make a heavenly combination.

My choice of music to quilt by is eclectic. I love upbeat, showy, florid music. My quilting needle moves with stately control to the "Triumphal March" from *Aida*. My needle is brazen and heroic as I listen to the "Toreador" song from *Carmen*. I feel majestic, as if I should rise and give the royal wave when I hear "Land of Hope and Glory."

I have taken to browsing through the bargain CD bins in the music stores, and I've unearthed some dandy quilting music. The blaring sounds of the Tiajuana Brass fill me with below-the-border energy. The mellow sounds of a Nat King Cole retrospective soothe me. Harry Belafonte pours warm gold into my soul.

I have to be careful which music I choose. When my Greek folk music twangs out across my quilt frame, I feel the desire to leap up and stamp about the room. Country line-dance music entices me to drop my needle, hook my thumbs in my belt loops and swing my feet and hips. Luckily, I quilt alone.

- - - - -

Last night, I found the ultimate quilt music. For $2.98, I bought a disc of Dixieland. As I sit and quilt and listen, the bass thumps, the trumpet wails, and the piano twangs. My hips rock in the chair, and my heel taps. My very soul moves with the beat. I find that my fingers are high-stepping, strutting across my quilt, and my quilting is spirited and free. Dixieland moves me; I sway to the sounds of "Go Down, Moses," my body moves to the wailing notes of "Go, Tell It on the Mountain," and I can promise you this: "When the Saints Go Marching In," I'm going to be there in that number, too, waving my quilting hoop and my needle.

License No. HK-428-27

The postman handed me a long, brown envelope this morning. Inside was a card which read, "Driver Services Division." It was my notice to renew my driver's license. Every four years, just before my birthday, this same form drops into my mailbox.

I've had my driver's license for a long, long time. Along with the regularity of the arrival of the renewal notice has been the repetition of the same old information printed in bold, black print by some impersonal computer. Ordinarily, I take my application card to the Examining Office. I squint through the little eye piece mounted on the counter to prove that I can still read the eye charts. I write out a check, and just as regularly my shiny, new plastic license arrives in the mail.

This morning I read my application card a bit more carefully than usual as I sipped my morning coffee. Number four on the unimpressive list of information stamped on the back of the card stands out from the rest. Number four is written in bold capital letters and it says, ENTER HEIGHT AND/OR WEIGHT CHANGES ONLY IF THEY EQUAL OR EXCEED TWO INCHES IN HEIGHT OR TEN POUNDS IN WEIGHT.

This set me to thinking. In fact, it set me scurrying back over the entire list of nine questions. I have never changed my "statistics" before. I have breezed merrily

- - - - -

through life assuming that nothing changes, that I do not change. This year, it is time to take inventory.

I am obviously not in mint condition, not like I was all those years ago when I first registered for my license. Weight: to be statistically honest, my weight change does not exceed ten pounds. But to be equally honest, my batting has shifted. It has slipped down a bit toward the foot. I am softer around the edges, a little more lumpy.

Eyes: blue; Hair: brown. Even "way back then" that was an unaesthetic description. Yet, these years later my eyes are still blue, my hair still brown. My colors are still quite bright. I am somewhat mellower, though. The glow, the fresh-air freckles have disappeared. I like to think that I have taken on a feeling of gracefulness that wasn't apparent when I was new.

Height: I don't think I've stretched or shrunk. I'd bet that if I stood up against the closet door frame with a yardstick, I'd make a mark just about where I did 35 years ago . . . that is, if I could pry myself out from under the quilt frame long enough to unbend. I have wrinkles. Fine quilting always makes lines and furrows. They add to the appeal. My fabric may be a bit worn at the edges. But there were times in my younger days that I came unravelled, too. Mostly my materials are still strong, my components function well together. I am pretty serviceable.

Over on the right side of the card is an address. It lists the same street, the same house number where I live today. But is it the same house? Back then, the paint was new, the shrubbery smaller. There was a tall pine tree in the front yard that went over in the big storm in '69. Inside the furniture is the same. The refrigerator stands exactly where every family member can find it, without even turning on the kitchen light. But caught in the shag of the rug are all of those pins that have disappeared over the years.

The rug has developed an interesting attribute. It stands higher in the middle under the quilt frame and it is ringed with a worn spot, trampled by all of the feet that have edged around it to get to the phone or out to the dinner table. My windows are dirtier. I'd rather quilt than do windows. My closets have changed functions and personalities. They hold fewer towels, coats and hats. They hold more fabric. The children's books have been packed away in boxes in the basement and my bookshelves display quilt manuals, quilt history books, quilt magazines. Now we have a variety of lamps with bright 100-watt bulbs parked about the house in every dark corner, and some not-so-dark corners. My quilt chair has had its bottom sat out. When I walk about this house now, the warmth of it reaches out to me and comforts me. All of the creating, the learning, the laughing fill it. It's the same address, but is it the same house?

- - - - -

I sip a second cup of coffee and I study those printed statistics. I will take my card to the examiner this afternoon. It will read that my hair is still brown and that I still live at the same address. The examiner will frown a bit and he will look at me carefully to be sure that it is really this same person who is applying. He will not see that I have changed, that everything around me has changed. How could he know that all of the handling, loving, and use have made me somewhat different.

He will stamp my card. He will take my check. In a few weeks my new license will come. It will read exactly as it has read all of these years.

Riding Lesson

When people show me their quilts, the ones they have pieced and quilted during long car trips, I am often amazed. I am equally amazed by people who can ride along in cars contentedly, with their hands folded quietly in their laps. I can do neither of these things.

Bill and I are about to drive off on a short excursion, just a day there and a day back. That's two whole days of just sitting, accomplishing nothing while the things I would love to be doing are piled up on my worktable back home. Bill will do most of the driving, but I certainly cannot sit in that passenger seat, gazing out the window idly. When I was a child, we used to count license plates or memorize Burma Shave signs. Do you remember Burma Shave signs? They said things like, "Don't put your elbow out so far. It might go home in another car." Such pertinent couplets were written out on four successive boards. They were staked at intervals along the highways and made the miles fun. Sometimes, back then; we also watched for gas stations with clean restrooms. Sometimes we poked a sister, or, at least, my sister poked me. I was much too nice to poke anyone. We couldn't read, since looking down made our stomachs queasy. Life is not much different now.

I am too old for license plate counting, and the Burma Shave signs have all been taken down. What's to do? When I work at home, I keep one or two good lamps blazing around me, and I sit in a quiet and protected atmosphere with my good scissors and fine, sharp needles right there beside me. When I am in the car, the light is mediocre at best, and the car vibrates and jiggles. My tools are always just out of reach, tucked into boxes on the floor or on the back seat. My workspace in the car is confining and elbow space is at a minimum. This is not a satisfying way for me to work.

I have finally come to grips with this quandary. It is impossible for me to do fine applique and piecing in the car, and a quilting hoop propped on the dashboard is a less-than-satisfying arrangement. So I embroider. I write messages and sign my name on quilt backs that I will use sometime, somewhere. I do simple embellishments on small quilt tops. My embroidery is not very elaborate. It is confined to stern stitching for outlining and writing, and now and then, a french knot. My french knots are barely adequate since they tend to dangle instead of pulling into tight little dots. My feather stitching, though, is quite acceptable. I like feather stitching for making simple vines and bushes. That is all the embroidery I know how to do, but it's all that I need, and riding in the car is the perfect time and place to do it.

So for this trip, we have packed the car with our folding chairs and our small suitcases and our lunches.

We have tucked in a thermos of ice water and road maps. I made sure we both had our dark glasses and sweatshirts. All those things are important. But the most important thing of all is my sewing kit and my tangle of embroidery floss. It's true what my mother always told me. She said, "Helen Louise, there is a time and a place for everything."

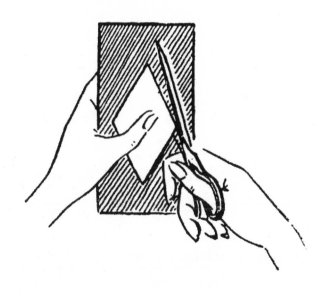

Let's Have Another Cup of Coffee

Every morning, the first thing I do is make the coffee. While Bill is poking around in the cereal drawer, I fill the carafe with water and pour it into the top of the coffee maker. Every morning, the water spills over the side and splashes on the floor. Every morning Bill says, "Would you like me to show you how to do that right?" And every morning I say, "No, thank you." Then I pull a paper towel off the roll and drop it onto the floor and blot up the water. The floor beneath the coffee maker is the cleanest place in the house.

I like making coffee that way. It's the way I've done it for years.

There are lots of things about my sewing that I have done the same way for years, too. There may be newer and easier methods for doing some of these things, but I have always done them in the same way, and I'm happy with them. For instance, the edges of the window curtains do not quite meet when I close them behind my sewing machine table at night. The closing mechanism would probably work again if I threaded a new cord through the fixture, but that takes time. When the sun comes up in the morning and shines into my eyes through the crack, I just reach into my pin dish, pick out a long pin, and pin the two sides of the curtain together.

My way works fine. I do it that way every morning. Have for years!

When I pick out basting threads and bits of badly sewn patchwork, I have a wastebasket right beside my knee to catch them. I drop those clingy threads and scraps *toward* that spot. The threads, of course, are electrostatically charged and cling to my fingers, landing on the floor or my jeans legs or my arms, but rarely in the wastebasket. I could pull the basket a little closer, I suppose. I could put a cup of water beside me to wet my fingers to foil all the static, but I don't. When I finish sewing, I crawl across the floor with my trusty lint picker-upper, gathering those errant threads before I vacuum. In that way, I can corral them before they get wrapped around the rolling brush on my vacuum cleaner. I do it this way every time. Have for years!

When I am working on a scrappy quilt, I begin carefully sorting through the fabrics in my cupboard. I lift the pieces out, one at a time, trying each fabric against the others I have selected. If satisfied, I drop it on top of a waiting stack on the floor. Sometimes, as I work, fabric falls out of the cupboard. I add that to the stack, too, or I simply push it to one side, out of the way. What I started to do carefully—picking and sorting fabrics into neat piles—turns into a wild conglomeration of yardage, scraps, and tatters of fabrics scattered all across the floor. With all those lovely colors and patterns spread out, I feel like an artist mixing her oil paints on a palette. I can shuffle through my stash and discover happy accidents, delightful combinations that might never have been found if I had planned my fabric choices more carefully. Years ago when I first got this cabinet for my material, every piece was folded flat, de-threaded, sorted by color, and neatly stored. Now it is utter confusion. My way might bother others, but I've done it like this for a long time.

Somebody somewhere said that you can't teach an old dog new tricks. I don't want to know new tricks. The old ones work just fine. In the same way that I find the feel of fabric and the glorious colors comforting, I find my old habits soothing. My friends have lovely new cutting tables and design walls. They have fancy filing cabinets and tricky tools. Their work spaces are orderly and dust free and everything is convenient, but my ways suit me just fine. I don't want to know another way to make coffee or to clean up my thread messes. There's something satisfying in my old habits. They are an integral part of me. I've always done these things this way. Have for years!

Six Delicious Flavors

"Ladies and gentlemen, this is the Jack Benny Program, brought to you by Jell-O—strawberry, raspberry, cherry, orange, lemon, and lime." Such was the grand introduction to that classic, old radio program. It was delivered with great flair and backed by the sound of a full orchestra. We kids would chant the "six delicious flavors" along with the announcer. It was a kind of mantra, and every time we came to the "orange" part, I would be delighted. I loved orange; I always have. It is autumn now, and the world outside my window is orange, and once again I am delighted.

I love orange sherbet and mandarin oranges, duck a l'orange, and orange juice. I love orange sunsets and orange zinnias, orange maple leaves and orange goldfish and orange quilts. Orange sparkles my heart.

My love of orange may have something to do with my physical makeup. I have freckles, and orange is a part of me. When I was five, my big brother would chase me, threatening to pull out my freckles "by the root." He scared the living daylights out of me, but he never caught me, and I never lost a freckle. Now, I cherish my orange spots and feel sorry for those people who have pure, flawless complexions with rosy cheeks. Age spots on people with flawless skin look like blotches. Mine just look like big orange freckles.

- - - - -

I needed orange back in the 1980s when I made my Marigold Quilt; then, it was nearly impossible to find that color fabric in stores.

Generally, the only thing available to a quilter was 36″-wide Halloween costume material. I gleaned everything that I could find in a variety of fibers and finishes that was remotely orange. Even then, the array was so meager that when I pieced my quilt, I extended my choices by using both sides of the fabrics. To this day, when people look closely at that quilt, they ask me, "Hey, do you know that you used the wrong side of that fabric?" And I say, "Of course, I doubled my options."

I am fully aware that all the world does not love orange like I do. Luckily, quilt shops are filled with other delicious flavors to tickle your taste buds. You might prefer the glorious choices in strawberry, raspberry, cherry, lemon, and lime. Those reds and yellows, blues, greens, and purples come in seemingly infinite tones and tints, nuances and styles that include ethnic prints, batiks, sunsets, and evening stars.

Amazingly, every color has its bright side and its gentle side; each can be sharp and tingling or quiet and calming. We often think of blues and greens as restful, but when you find a lustrous aqua or a glorious, vibrating electric blue, or a green that is jazzed up with threads of gold, it radiates with energy. The exciting thing about all of this is that we now have a choice between vivacity

- - - - -

or quiet, restful shades of the same hues. You can find them all on shop shelves. The menu there is tantalizing. Right next to one another, for example, might be the delicate, perfect pink of a gentle rose print, so fragile that it takes your breath away, and the hard, Day-Glo pink on a child's animal print. Just when you thought you knew what pink was, it becomes something different. And so it is with all of the colors—same flavors with tasty differences for all of us to sample.

When I walk into a quilt store, I might carry a scrap of paper with a precise list of what I need, such as exact measurements for fabric for borders or a backing. Yet when I leave, I always have something wonderful in my bag that I hadn't intended to buy. It's usually something delicious that I spotted high up on a shelf, something that caught my eye and tempted me, an unexpected treat. And for me, usually it is orange.

Four Days

We are only going away for four days, for goodness sakes. We decided to take this trip a month ago to fly out to California for a little R&R. So, a month ago we began planning. I worked day and night to get a quilt marked so that I could deliver it to my Wednesday Needleworkers for them to sew on. I scrubbed out pencil marks and made new ones for them to follow and I basted and wrote lengthy notes of explanation that probably nobody will read.

When that was ready, I began to work furiously on this State Fair quilt that I am making for one of the Great-Grandchildren, all that squinting at and digging into my stash and piecing and sorting and appliquéing and sewing and unsewing. I made such a mess that it took me one whole day this week to clean up my workroom. I have the quilt backing all pieced, now, and I will take that along on the trip to embroider the dedication on it and when I bring it home, I can sandwich it with the top and get it right into the quilt frame.

I cleaned the fridge. I washed the laundry. I sorted summer and winter clothes. I answered all the mail I had piled up on the dining-room table. I cleaned the disposal. I changed the sheets. I have been purely frantic. Bill is upstairs making out fancy schedules and routes. He is making lists of things he thinks we "might want to do," but like I said, we'll only be gone for four days, for goodness sakes.

This afternoon my frantic activity had coasted to a near stop. Everything seemed to be accomplished. So, I sat down with a project I have been playing with for a long time and I embroidered my name on it. That took up a couple of hours. I did a crossword.

The house is quiet. The new fabric for my stash that has been waiting to be washed is folded neatly and put away. The activity has been non-stop. It isn't like we have to the leave the house in perfect condition so that it will look nice enough to sell. It isn't like I'm never coming back. It isn't like we are coming home to a storm or a power outage or a dam that is about to burst. Like I said, for heavens sakes, it's only for four days.

Now I only need to pack.

I watch other quilters go away on trips and they seem to stay fairly calm. The most important thing to some of them is that they have their credit card and enough room in their suitcase left to pack any fabric they might find along the way and bring back. If they are going to take a workshop where they are going, they might pack tools and materials for that, though some quilters are so well schooled in this traveling business that they buy those sorts of things when they arrive. I watched one contingent of quilters drive off into the sunset, heading for a conference, with the car packed with popcorn, potato chips, and brownies.

- - - - -

We will be traveling by plane, and plane travel has evolved into a whole new science in these past couple of years. On one trip, I had to surrender my beloved Swiss Army knife to the security person. That made me very sad. My shampoo and toothpaste is neatly folded into my one-quart plastic zipper bag. I have my nightie in my tote bag over my shoulder in case my luggage gets sent to some far-off place by mistake or simply disappears forever. Nowadays, anything is possible, and it is impossible to prepare for all contingencies, but we are only going away for a little while.

I think that if you do this traveling enough, maybe the packing becomes automatic. Maybe you have a small bag already prepared with essentials like lipstick and a shower cap that you can just slip into your carry-on. Or maybe you just consider what is most important and let the rest take care of itself. Obviously, I want to leave a neat house behind me, so that I can concentrate on the dirty laundry I must do when I bring it home. I want to be able to walk into a clean, sweet-smelling house without discovering that I forgot to take out the garbage before I left. I don't want to find that I forgot to pay a bill that was due a couple of days ago. I want my obligations taken care of, the things I promised others—like the quilt block that needs to be finished or the library books that need to be returned. I want to come home "Rested & Recreated" so that I can tie right back into this stash of things I want to do for and with my family and friends. Four days can be a wonderful, fresh, jam-packed time and like a good Girl Scout, I want to "be prepared." I have tried to make everything just right, so I need to keep a level head. I must stay focused while I am packing for this trip, even if it is, for goodness sakes, only four days.

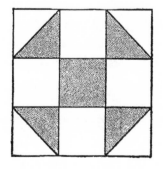

Tut Tut!

I have fallen victim to the Pyramid Syndrome. Today at the shoe store, I discovered that I no longer wear a shoe with a AAA width. The salesman slipped a little tan pump on my foot that was only a double A. To add to my astonishment, it was a size 8. I have always worn a size 7½. This shoe fit beautifully.

It is time to take stock of myself! Always before I have worn a size 12 blouse. Now I look better in a size 8. My skirts have changed from a size 12 to a 14. Radical shifts are taking place in my shape, all downward.

I am standing in front of my mirror and studying myself. My shoulders are seeping into my bust, my bust slipping into my waist. My waist is definitely shifting into my hips, and my hips sliding into my thighs. I believe my knees are getting heavier. The calves of my legs seem to be settling into my ankles, and as I have said, my feet are spreading out to support the entire structure.

I realize that all this shifting has to do with aging. Everyone is getting older, even my grandchildren: that doesn't bother me. I figure that I have at least forty more good quilting years ahead of me. I intend to attain the *Guinness Book*'s record as the World's Oldest Quilter. No, I don't mind the getting-older part. What I hate is the cost of the new clothes needed to cover this changing body shape. I can wear my quilting/jogging suits for most occasions, but sweat pants are not exactly *de rigeur* for candlelight dinners at expensive restaurants, meeting dignitaries, or attending weddings. Some occasions require a little class.

Aging quilts are another story. They can get old, lumpy, wrinkly, and spotty and we still love them. If they shrink up a bit, we fold them across the bottom of the bed or display them on quilt racks. If they have stretched out of shape (or even if they were originally made that way), nobody even notices when they are smoothed out across a bed,

I remember one time when I was making my college-aged daughter's bed to help her out during finals week. A tattered scrap of quilt fell out from under her pillow, and she was embarrassed that I had discovered her secret. She simply couldn't let go of her childhood treasure, no matter how gray and shreddy it was.

When babies are grown and their crib quilts are no longer a useful size, we hang the little quilts on the wall or tuck them away in a drawer for the next generation.

Friends have shown me narrow, cot-sized quilts on which they have sewn dust ruffles so that they would cover wider beds. Nobody in his or her right mind would discard a lovely quilt because it is the wrong size!

I have salvaged the faded loveliness of an old quilt found beside the road by making it into a crib quilt.

- - - - -

I have spread a gentle old quilt across a tabletop and covered it with a sheet of clear plastic to use it as a holiday tablecloth. Everyone loves quilts, misshapen and soft as they may become. Aging is not a problem,

Alas, my body has fallen victim to the Pyramid Syndrome. No amount of diet or exercise will outsmart Father Time. My quilts, I hope, will develop a different Pyramid Syndrome, piling up higher and higher as I count them and love them. Even if they are saggy-baggy, soft and dumpy, I will keep saving them, sorting them, savoring them, and stacking them, ever upward.

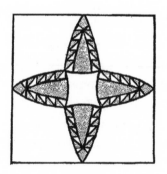 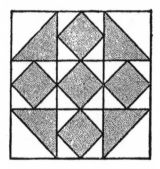

When All Else Fails

I have always made jokes about being inept on all machines except my sewing machine. Fancy ovens, electric mixers, and typewriters all hate me. Anything with a moving part is a threat. Up until now, I have been content to do everything, slowly by hand, sewing excepted. I have bought the simplest equipment so that I need not thread my way through the mysteries of modern technology.

Now, suddenly, at this time in my life, everything I own is breaking, and I find that it is impossible to buy anything simple. Everything comes with a manual, usually written by someone who uses English as a second language.

When I went shopping for my new car last week, I was looking for a "bare bones" car. I told the salesman, "No options." He informed me patiently that "options" are not things you can opt to buy. They are the things included in the car that are listed separately for the purpose of merchandising. The only alternative was to buy a car that simply switched on and ran when you turned the key. Since there were a couple of modest amenities that I felt were civilized, it meant that I had to buy the whole "package." When the car arrived, the salesman sat in it with me for half an hour. He told me which buttons to push and which pedals to tromp and which dials to turn. When he was through, I knew nothing more than how to turn the key in the ignition to start the car. I ride with the manual on the seat and when I need to turn on the lights, I pull over to the side of the road and look up "Lights."

My husband is an engineer, but he sits cross-legged on the floor, poring over the VCR manual. He is trying to understand how to tape a quilt show for me because I am going to be away during the day.

My rotary cutter came without any manual at all. If you take it apart to put in a replacement blade, the little drawing on the back of the blade package tells you nothing at all. There is a curly little piece of metal that serves as a washer, and once you have your cutter apart, blade inserted, and begin putting all those round things back in place, it is impossible to figure out whether that washer should curl out or in toward the cutter or if it makes any difference at all.

I have manuals attached to everything. My washing machine has a little metal pocket on the back side just to hold the manual, though everything that goes into that machine gets washed on warm/full load/15 minutes. By the time I have wrestled with all my other equipment, I don't have the patience for creative laundry.

A few pieces of equipment around my house are in their death throes. I think I had better replace them immediately and hope the new ones will last forever. I

- - - - -

need to be equipped with existing tools in case things get any more complicated. I'm not sure I can deal with "bigger and better" tools and manuals.

In spite of my struggles with current inventive minds and their corresponding literary output, every time I go to the quilt store, I wander over to the rack that has all the pokers and dabbers and needles and rulers and templates, and I rifle through them. "What's new?" I always ask. I have a workroom full of what's-new things, some of which I will cheerfully give away, some of which I would cry if I should lose them. I cannot resist the products of creative quilters' brains, gadgets that let me do undreamed-of things.

Some have no directions at all, some I have to play with. Some have little dotted lines and diagrams to lead me. I suppose that the thing that makes most of these tools easier for me to use is that the directions are written in my first language, "Quiltese." I'm really good at it and I speak it fluently. I have great difficulties with words like "cursor," "code," "status," "function," and "delete." Octane ratings and timing-belt directions baffle me. I know, however, exactly what "mark," "cut," "miter," "turn," "seam," and "apply" mean. "Tack" and "trim" have musical sounds. "Backstitch" and "bias" are lovely words. I have no problem understanding and translating directions written in Quiltese. It is first and foremost my language. It is the true Romance language.

- - - - -

Darn It!

My great-grandson is going to get a storytelling quilt from me soon. The quilt has puppies all over it—puppies in baskets, puppies chewing on bones, and puppies tugging on ropes. I call it a storytelling quilt because I made a matching bookbag to go with it and filled it with children's books about dogs.

The top took a good deal more creativity than I had anticipated because the original puppy print was predominantly tans and grays. It needed to be zapped up to make the little boy happy. I pieced in reds and greens and yellows and blues to frame the puppies, and I set it all with a steely blue to make the colors jump for joy. The quilt top sparkled.

Last night, I worked late on piecing the backing for this quilt. When I made the top, I set aside the big piece of leftover puppy fabric to make the backing. It was long enough, but not wide enough to fit the quilt. My plan was to cut that big, printed piece right down the middle and insert a long, ladder-like strip of colored bars made from colorful scraps from the top. That color ladder would be enough to enlarge the backing piece and add, I hoped, sparkle to the backing, too.

When I cut the materials for the ladder insert, I used every snippet. Nothing was left but the threads and snibbles that were strewn across my workroom floor.

Only a 3″ scrap of steely blue poking out over the edge of my wastebasket.

When I had finished cutting and sewing the ladder, it looked exactly as joyful as I had hoped. I was exhilarated. The clock on the mantel read midnight, and I knew I should go to bed. I knew that, but I was excited, too excited to sleep before the finishing touches were done. I spread my big remaining piece of doggy fabric on my cutting board, and with my trusty rotary cutter, cut it right straight down the middle. I put my cutter down with a flourish and cut a 3″ gash in my backing.

This is not the first time, and probably won't be the last, that I have worked too late at night and in my enthusiasm, have done more harm than good to my quilt. This time, though, I truly had no resources left to mend my error. There was no puppy fabric. There was no fabric left from the ladder.

It is a humbling thing when you have to admit that you have made a stupid mistake. I scrambled about on the floor picking up snippets and scraps, and once I was nose to nose, so to speak, with the wastebasket, that piece of steely blue fabric looked back at me. I shaped it carefully, trimming the corners into curves and turning them under smoothly. I appliqued that patch— a plain, ordinary, unimaginative, steely blue patch—to the back of that little quilt. It was slightly askew, but it was neat.

- - - - -

I'd like to think I've learned a lesson from this quilt, but I know that I will probably make a similar mistake again. Even though I know that fatigue makes me unreliable and rash, I still stay up late. There is something about finishing a quilt that sends me into spasms of delight. It makes me careless and carefree. I just wish I were sensible enough to avoid the midnight mayhem and simply celebrate in the morning.

Chapter 3

COMMON
THREADS

When I'm Calling You

I have a cell phone. Bill calls me on it when he stops at the grocery store to ask what I need, or he calls me to let me know when he's on his way home from a late meeting. It's an easy way to communicate. It saves me worry, and I enjoy the convenience and the immediacy of it.

Having this means of communication so close at hand reminds me of the pulley network my neighborhood girlfriends and I rigged up when we were in the sixth grade. I had a string tied around the metal handle on my bedroom window. The string went out over the roof of the porch next door, wrapped around my friend Suey's window handle, and came back again to my house. It had been quite a feat to put up this arrangement. We tied one end of the string to a rock, and Suey, standing in the garden below, threw the rock up in the air again and again until I, leaning out my upstairs window, caught it. We tied the two ends of the string together to complete the loop. Then we could attach paper notes to the string and pull it until the notes moved from one window to the other across the space between our houses. We waved to each other and read the important, secret messages. We could have shouted them to each other, but that would have been no fun at all.

Eventually, that pulley system went all over the neighborhood. One string went to Pricilla's and one to Betsy's and one to Betty's. Betty's leg of the journey was difficult because she lived across the road, and the string sagged and kept getting caught on passing busses.

The point is that we were all tied together. We talked to each other, we communicated, and we laughed. It was an adventure. It was just like a quilting bee.

Every week when I go off to stitch with my Needleworkers, I look forward to the morning as much for the pleasure of sewing as for the joy of sharing. Just as we neighborhood girls laughed when we shared secret notes, we quilters laugh together, too. We share little familiarities and the satisfaction of being friends.

We recently had a new member join us. Lucy, a lady from Africa, came to our group because she hoped she could improve her English by listening to us talk. I asked her slowly and distinctly if she understood what we were all saying.

She laughed and replied, "I do not understand a word anybody says." She was bewildered by our inside jokes and our Americanisms. But now, after she has joined us week after week to stitch bindings on her quilts and to listen to our repartee, her English is improving. She can follow our chatter. She is part of the current of our lives.

- - - - -

That's exactly what a quilting bee is. It's a time when quilters plug in to the currents of the lives of those around them and become part of those currents. Maybe this is the most important part of quilting.

When others see quilters sitting together, do you suppose that all they see is a group of people sewing? Do other people understand that we are sharing something more than needles and thread, that we are sharing ideas and concerns and affections? The bond among women who sew together is strong. Although Lucy still says very little as she stitches, she smiles, and sometimes she even laughs. We know that as she binds another side of her quilt, she understands about our children and about our new recipes and about our sick pets. As she shifts in her chair and turns the quilt to the next edge, she laughs with us. Lucy is on our wavelength.

As a child, I felt secure in that loop of pulley strings and friendships. As a grown woman, I feel secure in this circle of quilters as we share our lives.

Chit Chat

Do you talk to yourself? I do, all the time. My mother used to say that either I was very rich or very mad. Psychologists think they have an answer. They say that people who work in solitary situations talk to themselves. Well, I am not mad; I certainly am not rich. But I find myself discussing things with myself all the time.

When I am here in my workroom, I have easy conversations. I sort things out in my head and chat as I work. "Let's see. I wonder if it will fit this way?" You know the sort of conversation because you do it all the time yourself, don't you?

It's embarrassing, though, when I am in the supermarket and find myself talking to the breakfast cereal. "Let's see, where are the cornflakes? Aha, here they are! I wonder what's on the back of the box. Hmmm! I can get Free Miracle Stickers inside or this brand over here has Funny Rings." Then, I look up to see a fascinated spectator. I have had observers stand in hushed awe as if I were a phenomenon akin to Halley's comet. I always feel silly, but a few aisles over I find myself chatting with my favorite spaghetti sauce, and the butcher thinks I am rather funny when I discuss price and weight labels with packages of cut-up chicken.

When I see someone else muttering to herself, I think what a strange lady she is, and then I realize that I do exactly that myself. I remember, as a small child, walking down to the corner with my friends to stand and wait for a man to come out of his house so that we could see him talking to himself. In our youth and inexperience we used to call him "goofy."

Those of us creative, intelligent people who talk to ourselves are keeping an oral journal, and if there were someone else around to jot down our mumblings (God forbid!), they would document the joys and sorrows, the stories of our lives. What lovelier words have been uttered than, "Ahhhh, I found it"? Or, on the other side of the coin, "Ouch, so that's where I lost my needle!" What about. "Whoops! All over the floor!"

Words for your diary could sound like this:

SOUNDS OF DISTRESS

"They tell me if I spit on it, it will come out."

"There has to be a better light than this. Maybe it would help if I washed my glasses."

"I wonder what I could applique over that one?"

SOUNDS OF CREATIVITY

"Those colors sure did strange things, but you know, I rather like what happened. I think I'll go along with it."

"I tried to draw it but it sure doesn't look like a

rabbit. Well, yes, it does, too. It's my kind of rabbit, my own rabbit."

"That's absolutely the last scrap of that material, and I'm short. I wonder what it will look like if I substitute this odd little piece?"

SOUNDS OF JOY

"Oh, wow! Here's some of the fabric that I've looked for all over town."

"What an absolutely smashing idea. I'm going to try it."

AND THE SWEETEST SOUNDS OF ALL

"Whoopee! It's finished."

Griselda

(THE ANCIENT ROMAN WOMAN WHO BECAME
THE UNIVERSAL EMBODIMENT OF PATIENCE)

I am a woman of extraordinary patience. I have learned
patience through my quilting. Patience is required,
since making a quilt is not a fast, instant-gratification
kind of thing. First of all, it requires the time to dream
a dream. Then, with that dream in mind, we embark
on all of that cutting and stitching. Certainly putting
on the binding with those tiny stitches, round and
round, tucking and turning to make a perfect edge,
develops persistency. We are rewarded in the end with
our dream fulfilled.

The patience needed for quilting doesn't hold a
candle to that needed for using automated telephone-
answering devices. I have said frequently that machines
hate me. (All of them, that is, but my sewing machine.)
In general, if I use machines, I do so with great
caution. I approach them slowly and with care. I read
the instructions meticulously: "a. Turn lever, b. Push
button, c. Wait." Each of these movements is done with
thoughtful consideration. I have also learned to use a
screwdriver, with some success, to adjust a machine.
I even can operate a microwave oven after several
reprogram attempts. I know my limitations, however,

and I would never think of setting a VCR to tape my favorite quilt show. That is why I married a mechanically adept man.

Nothing has prepared me, though, for automated answering services. I am probably old-fashioned, but I do prefer to talk to a human being. I admit to this prejudice. When I call a telephone number that is connected to an automated device, I am instructed by a mechanical voice to make a choice and press 1, 2 or 3, and then that request is followed by a second set of choices and a third set, ad infinitum. When my call is answered by one of these machines, apprehension fills me. The inexorable droning of choices is, for me, like the sound of chalk screeching on a blackboard. Furthermore, one of these extended sessions over long-distance phone lines evokes visions of a meter somewhere in the recesses of the phone company spinning around and around, clocking up dollars on my next bill.

When a mechanical voice answers, and I push the buttons as I am told to do; inevitably, something goes wrong. I never have any idea of what it is. Somewhere between "Push 3" and the next set of demands, something inexplicable happens. Perhaps my hand hits something irrelevant as it drifts across the telephone buttons. Whatever it is, I do it. When I realize that I have done this wrong thing, I hang up, redial, and start all over.

- - - - -

I have discovered that if I wait patiently, sometimes, after the routine has run its course, a real, live person will pick up the phone. Maybe the rest of the world has learned to deal successfully with automated answering, but I, in my ineptness, have dragged a customer service representative away from her cup of coffee to solve a problem that should be simple (in fact, was simple before automated answering).

Even if I have made the effort to tiptoe through the sequences of button pushing, I am never sure if I have, in fact, actually communicated my information. I made a telephone transfer to the bank the other night, and I felt uneasy about the experience. The final recorded message was, "We are sorry but no customer service representative is available to you during these hours." I thought they were apologizing to me for not letting me talk directly to a human being. Several days later I called the bank to inquire about the transfer and discovered that my automatic transaction had never been registered. I would have been in big trouble if my electricity check or my mortgage check had bounced, but imagine if my check for my quilt books order had bounced!

My quilt guild has put one of these automated systems on its phone. Using it will test my patience. I have, therefore, made this resolve. I will not push any more numbers. I will wait patiently, instead for

- - - - -

a live human being to answer the phone. I won't be embarrassed about interrupting this person, taking her away from some meaningful activity, like writing the minutes of the last meeting or stapling the newsletter. I will wait until I can talk to this breathing, thinking person, who will be considerably easier to communicate with than a computerized, synthesized, impersonal voice. Patience is virtuous. I am a patient quilter. Being a quilter, it seems, is good training for life in the mechanical, technically oriented twenty-first century.

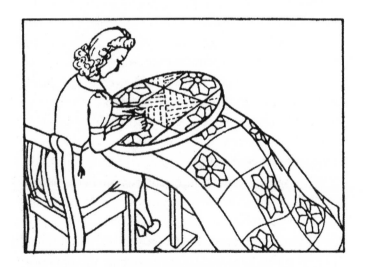

Tuna Melt

It was a big mistake. I should never have asked. Dinners at my house have gotten pretty bland of late. I was looking for something different to have for supper. Somehow, the idea of tuna melts slipped into my mind. I searched through cookbooks, dug through my file drawer, and even went on the Internet. Tuna melts are so common, it appears, that cookbook writers add little twists and turns to make their own recipes unique. I made a list of all the various flavors, nuances, and textures. I was well armed when I went off to my Wednesday morning quilt group. Those ladies are great cooks with discriminating palates. They are a wonderful source of culinary expertise. "Okay," I said to them, "I need your opinion. If you were going to make tuna melts, would you use sesame buns, onion buns, or multigrain bread?"

"Whatever I happen to have in my bread drawer," came each of their replies.

"Do you use cucumber or green pepper or celery?"

"Whatever is in the refrigerator," was the answer.

This was no fun. I needed definites. I wanted opinions from experienced people. I wanted specific directions.

"How about dressing?" I asked. "Do you use mayo, salad dressing, or french dressing?" Again, their replies were the same. "Use whatever you have."

Cheese was another "whatever." Cheese was a matter of personal preference—sharp cheddar for bite, mozzarella for texture, or processed slices for convenience.

I was no further ahead than when I began. The answers were always, "Whatever works." I needed measurements, brand names, and specifics. In other words, I wanted somebody to give me a kit or at least a pattern. I was truly frustrated.

At this point, one of the other quilters handed me a quilt top she'd made with two small slits she had accidentally cut into it. She wanted to know how she could fix it, and my first inclination was to say, "Just dampen the edges with Fray Chek or fabric glue and pull the slits together. Whatever works!" But I stopped myself. I realized that whether you are a beginning tuna-melt maker or a less-experienced quiltmaker, whatever works puts a lot of stress on the uninitiated. I took the top and carefully touched the edges of the slits with a faint bit of fabric glue on the tip of a darning needle, just enough to seal the vulnerable ends of the fibers. Then I drew the edges together with fine, firm stitches. I think it helped her to see, firsthand, how to do it. I have been mending boo-boos for so long, it could have been easy to be flippant, but this quilter needed guidance.

When I got home this afternoon, I began to prepare the sandwiches. I opened cans of tuna and drained off

- - - - -

the water. I chopped up a stalk of celery that I happened to have. I was ridiculously nervous about preparing this mundane meal, something of so little consequence. I needed somebody to hold my hand and help me along. I mixed in the mayonnaise. The mixture seemed a little dry so on a whim, I shook a couple of blobs of french dressing into it. This wasn't so hard! I began to feel a bit confident and maybe even creative.

Like beginning quilting classes, there should be beginning tuna-melt classes. They would eliminate the stress and strain of starting out. Tenderfoot quilters and neophyte chefs need encouragement. My cooking/quilting ladies sent me home with enough gentle guidance and direction to give me the confidence to be inventive. Please, please, all of you super-wonderful, highly experienced quilters, have patience with novice quilters. Help them. Show them how. Nurture them. Before your very eyes, "beginning tuna-melt quilters" can turn into superb chefs and master patchworkers.

Punch Drunk

For a long, long time, I've collected needles in a clear plastic circular sewing-machine needle case. It has little access holes on the outer rim that open one at a time when you rotate it. I can't remember where I got it originally, but it is handy, and I've filled its compartments with needles for sewing leather, denim, wovens or knits, and, of course, cotton.

I'd been making triangles of fabric into flowers. I drew little, quick-triangle squares onto lavender material, layered it with a piece of green leaf fabric, and then sat down to stitch them together, back and forth with diagonal lines across the squares. Strangely, my fine fabric seemed to be amazingly tough. My needle was snagging lavender threads and punching them in loops through the two layers of fabric. At my cutting board, after I cut apart the patchwork units, I had to use my little thread-snagger device to neaten the wounds and repair the blemishes. I was able to save the project, but whatever was the matter with my sewing machine?

Some days later, my local fabric shop had a special on canvas chairs that fold up and fit neatly into over-the-shoulder tote bags. When Bill and I ventured out to our first summer street festival armed with these chairs, it became quite clear why the chairs were so cheap. The carrying cases were made of flimsy fabric with no reinforcing on the seams. "Never fear," I told Bill, "help is here! I shall mend these covers and make them sturdy with my trusty machine and my assortment of specialized needles."

So I found a piece of scrap leather and trimmed it into neat patches with rounded corners. Then I unfastened the standard, everyday needle that was in my sewing machine. I found a leather needle in my handy-jim-dandy needle case from some long-forgotten project and inserted it into the socket of the machine. For safekeeping, into my pincushion went the regular needle I had first taken out. I heard a popping noise.

"That's odd," I thought, "my pincushion must have something gummy or hard inside." I pulled the needle out and poked it in again, several times. It popped each time. The needle was dull. Rather than wrestle with it ever again, I threw it away.

I began to wonder about the other needles in my handy caddy. Some of them had been stored there for years. I decided I should test them all, and like a voodoo priestess, I extracted those discolored, ancient needles one at a time, and stuck them into the heart of my pincushion. The needles were all "punchy."

Over the years, I've carefully stored needles I had used for an assortment of sewing projects, everything from filmy, lacy slips and nighties made from needle-blunting manmade fibers to bags made by sewing patchwork blocks together and stitching tough seatbelt strapping onto them to make the handles. These needles were obviously no longer usable. My sainted mother, as thrifty as she was, would have been shocked to see me as, one by one, I threw out my entire collection of these old standbys and replaced them with a whole new supply.

Today I am sewing more half-square triangles, this time to make tiny, yellow flowers. My sewing machine is threaded with a brand new, medium-weight needle for woven fabric, and it is bobbing up and down smoothly, flying across my work as if it were stitching on soft butter. The sight is sweet, the stitching is precise, and I am elated. Life is wonderful! Sometimes extravagance is good for the soul. The simple things in life, like sharp needles for instance, can be glorious. The luxury of tossing out clunky needles and nicked rotary cutter blades and snarled spools of thread is good.

We all have too little sewing time to let quilting challenges become quilting chores. We become sour and dogged and apathetic. Quilting should be pleasant. It should be satisfying. We can jump-start our enthusiasm in simple ways. Sometimes a fat quarter of a dazzling fabric can do it, and sometimes all it takes is a shiny, new needle.

- - - - -

Who Is the Fairest One of All?

The water in the shower this morning was deliciously hot. It slithered over my head and ran down my shoulders. I stood in it until the hot water tank ran cold. Then, wrapped with a thick, soft towel around my torso and a turban-style towel on my head, I stepped over the side of the tub and glanced at myself in the mirror above the sink.

"My word," I thought. "Hot showers are good for you. Look! The wrinkles are gone. No worry lines! Your skin looks so soft and young. Why you look as if you were thirty-five."

I was looking into a mirror covered with soft, glistening steam. I did not have my glasses on.

Now, I can tell Snow White, "That mirror lies."

When I opened the bathroom door and the cool air flooded in, the mist trickled down the mirror and disappeared. I put on my glasses. There I was, looking back at myself, looking just like I did yesterday. I did not look like I was thirty-five.

Nevertheless, I am all in favor of magic mirrors. Mine made me feel as if I were wonderful, lovely, young. The glory of it made my spirit beautiful.

It's the same way with some of the quilts that my friends bring to share with me. On rare occasions, someone rings my front doorbell with an astonishing, spectacular old quilt. When we have laid out a sheet on my living room floor and my friend has spread out her quilt on it, my hand pauses above the quilt in awe, and I always ask, "May I touch it?"

Often my visitor brings a gently faded quilt that her mother or her grandmother has made. Perhaps its maker was a favorite aunt. The quilt will likely be a Dresden Plate or a Grandmother's Flower Garden. Sometimes the stitches will be minute; often they are toenail catchers. Sometimes the quilts are flawless and unused; sometimes they are worn with use. Always, always she will describe the "miracle" of the quilt, its maker, its making, its life. Always, always the quilt is beautiful, always loved.

The wrinkles of the quilt, the lines, the age marks have disappeared in the mist of the mirror of her eyes, and who am I to say that this is not the most wonderful quilt ever made?

After all, "Mirror, mirror on the wall, which IS the fairest of them all?"

Shape Up or Ship Out

At a quilt convention recently, I shared a cafeteria table with two young quilters. As I munched my English muffin with marmalade and drank a cup of coffee, I eavesdropped shamelessly. I was mesmerized.

These women talked of barbells and of the "challenge" of weightlifting. They compared exercise equipment and schedules. I have always thought of women weight-lifters as oily ladies in bikinis with arms and legs ballooning grotesquely to exaggerated proportions. I've seen them on TV, and in my mind they are sort of a cross between the fabled greased pig at the county fair and the man on the comic book back cover who appears under the title: "I was a 97-pound weakling until. . . ."

Here I sat, not only eye to eye, but hip to hip with two women weight-lifters—and they were quilters. They were not bulgy. They were not strange. They were gorgeous. Their chests were exactly right, their arms firm and shaped to perfection. Their trim little waists gave way to well-molded hips. Their faces glowed with health.

I have made all sorts of excuses for my body. It resembles a warm molded Jello. I have thought this was probably the state of the art—advancing age. I have actually considered that perhaps my body was like a giant water balloon, only filled with coffee. Certainly my shape has nothing to do with the fact that I stitch and snip most of the hours of every day. Lack of activity can have no bearing, surely, on my shape.

Let's face it! I do not look like those two lovely quilters. To be honest, I didn't look like those two ladies thirty-five years ago when I was their age. Amazingly enough, they have found a way in their lives to do *two* things. They quilt *and* they exercise. That demolished my excuse, that I simply do not have the extra time.

My husband, Bill, goes to the YMCA at 6:30 in the morning to exercise. He climbs out of bed while I snooze and disappears into the morning mist. When he reappears in time for breakfast, he is bright-eyed. His cheeks glow. He is vibrant. I hate to admit it, but as I sit, sagging over my cup of coffee, he is becoming trimmer and handsomer.

One day he invited me to join him and take part in a wives' program. I told him frankly, "Bill, I detest exercise. The idea of getting out of a warm bed at 6 in the morning to go out into the cold world and exercise fills me with terror."

Yet each day he looks fitter and happier, and each day my hips spread a little more. It would be nice, 'tis true, to be a bit more shapely. I would enjoy looking trim and firm and being absolutely adorable, but I cannot in my wildest dreams imagine myself lifting barbells. Still, a few toe-touches and maybe a push-up or two might do wonders for me. I might even lose a few inches around the hips. At the next quilters' convention I would be sleek and slender and I might have a bit of healthy bloom in my own cheeks.

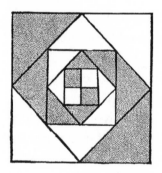 

Let Them Eat Cake

I've just come home from my guild's annual quilt show where I was staggered by the visual banquet. All of the ingredients of a lavish repast were there with every sort of flavor and vibrant color in row after row of beautifully displayed quilts. Truly, this show had something to please everyone's palate.

I think, however, that if I were a millionaire and could have anything I wanted, I would like to cook up my own, personal dream quilt show. For this fantasy, I would arrange for different quilts to be hung on successive days so that I could enjoy a limited number, say around fifty splendid ones, each day. The quilts would be displayed so that I could see them straight-on as well as from the back. I would be able to take pictures directly and effortlessly with an uninterrupted view. All of the quilts in my pictures would have lovely straight edges. At my show, I, as the millionaire princess, would be allowed to touch, feel, and flip each quilt to explore its splendid details. A limited number of quilter friends would be invited to view them with me, so that we could "ooh" and "aah" together and discuss and dispute each piece. Of course, my friends would stand behind me, never getting between me and the quilts. One needs friends at a quilt show to talk with and to celebrate. Like banquet guests, we would savor every course together.

I think that three days would be a perfect length for this show—three days of new quilts each day, three days of total indulgence. And during this flight of fancy, I could go to my quilt show any time I pleased. Even in the middle of the night, if I should wake, I would be able to go and look at whatever detail or technique that would not let me go back to sleep. I would have the hard, unrelenting concrete floor of the usual auditorium covered with lush, resilient carpeting. I remember seeing a picture of the tent in Africa where Queen Elizabeth stayed when she went on safari. Oriental rugs were laid on the ground for her, and I think that at my quilt show they would be nice, too. They would be in deep reds and blues. Nothing flashy, so they would not interfere or compete with the beauty of the quilts!

Lunch break would be in a fragrant garden where the sun would shine. My friends and I would discuss the quilts as we drank our coffee and nibbled on potato chips and Reuben sandwiches made with warm, creamy French dressing. You see, since this is my party, I would get to order the food.

The vendors would cut and fold two-yard lengths of the best fabrics for me. I would always be the first in line at the cash register, and one of my friends would carry my bundles for me.

In this, my dream feast, I would determine the menu. There would be small, witty quilts for appetizers, large

- - - - -

solid statements for the entrée, innovative experimental pieces for the salad course, and vivid flourishes for dessert.

Alas, I am no millionaire. I have no special privileges. I shall have to go to quilt shows just like everybody else. But, that's really not such a terrible thing either.

How Sweet It Is!

Birthdays should be special. They represent another year of loving, laughing, living, and lasting. Sometimes, over the years, I have been so involved with diapers and PTA and trips to doctors' offices that as I climbed into bed at night I've realized, "My goodness! It was my birthday, and I forgot it."

Not so this year. This year was a milestone birthday, and Bill announced that it should be celebrated properly. He made reservations for us at a gourmet restaurant that sits beside a lake in a small town nearby. I dressed up for the occasion—that means that I wore my lacy blue outfit that I save for quilt banquets—and we headed out into the soft, warm spring twilight to have our dinner.

At the restaurant, we were seated at a table with white linens and sparkling crystal and leather-covered menus. Of course, I had lobster; Bill always orders steak for special affairs. We ate leisurely as the twilight lengthened into evening, and I felt luxurious and overfed.

As the waitress carried away our dinner plates, Bill said, "You will have dessert, won't you?"

"Good heavens!" said I. "I am absolutely stuffed. I can't eat another bite."

"You *will* have dessert," said Bill. At that moment, the kitchen door opened and out came our waitress carrying a flaming birthday cake.

This was not your ordinary kind of birthday cake. Bill had gone to an upscale grocery store and conferred with the bakery chef. He had taken along an enlarged picture of my flower shop quilt, which is my favorite. Somehow, the chef transferred a perfect image of my quilt onto a thin sheet of sugar. This piece of culinary art then went to the restaurant pastry chef, who built a remarkable cake around it. The cake had all the tiniest details, from the little flowers made of hearts, to the ivy climbing up the bricks outside the flower shop window, to the scalloped red-and-white striped canopy at the top. Across the cake, the chef had written "Flowers to Helen" and had trimmed the edges with fluted cream frosting. People came from around the room to see my cake. The diners and waiters oohed and aahed. I blew out the candles.

I couldn't bear to cut that cake. Instead I saved it. I took it on Wednesday to share with my favorite people, my Wednesday Quilters. That's what a birthday cake is for, to share with your favorite friends. I wish you could have been there with us—you would have loved it! Now, every crumb is gone and all that's left is the memory of the joyful sharing of this sweetest, most beautiful birthday surprise that ever was.

Heavenly Days

Bill and I have the same astrological sign. We are both Taurus the Bull, though we are so different it is hard to find a single similarity. I know that variations in personality are attributed to the rising or the falling or the coming or the going or the in-betweening of the stars in the heavens at that gasp in time which is the moment that each of us was born. It's just as well that Bill and I are so different. I couldn't stand to be married to someone just like me, which is a good point in Bill's favor.

There is one characteristic, however, in which we are so much the same that it is frightening. True to the name of Taurus, we are both as stubborn as that proverbial bovine in the sky. But, we do not lock horns, and we react to problems differently. While Bill dissects and discusses, I leap to a quick solution and put it out of my mind. Then, as Bill discourses on the whys and wherefores of the situation, I am the Queen of Silence while I sit quietly and mentally design my next quilt.

Not so, when I am in the midst of quilters. What is it about them that energizes me? When I am huddled in a group at a meeting, seated around a quilt frame in a community center, or hunting through a friend's stash for a fabric need, I find that I cannot stop the flow of words. I babble. I gush.

Quilters, in general, are a gregarious bunch. The noise at my guild meeting resounds from the concrete-block walls of the hall much like it must have sounded at the Tower of Babel. My quilt group begins its meeting with Show and Tell. The anticipation of seeing new quilts is probably the only thing that can quiet the noise echoing in that room. Why do quilters become so energized when we are together? Are we stirred by the sense of community? The excitement of seeing friends? The comfort of being among others who share our passion? The thrill of seeing new creative triumphs? The aura of color? The feel of fabric?

There are guilds across this country that have members who do not quilt. Generally, we refer to these nonquilters as Quilt Appreciators. I wonder if actually they are Quilter Appreciators, which is, I think, a good thing to be. What is healthier for the mind and better for the soul than being among quilters watching their positive energy as it swirls around quilt gatherings?

Some tell St.-Peter-and-The-Pearly-Gate jokes involving quilters struggling up the gold stairs with their needles and quilt projects. If I climb those heavenly stairs and St. Peter meets me at the gate and asks me to come in, he may want to know with whom I will choose to spend eternity. I will tell him, "Quilters." Don't misunderstand me! I love my Bill who has not the foggiest idea of how to sew a ¼-inch seam. He is a

- - - - -

stubborn orator and a celestial bull-headed sort of guy. I have no intention of shutting him out of my paradise; the solution to this problem is quite simple. So that he qualifies for my special heaven, I just have to teach my husband how to quilt!

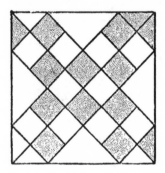 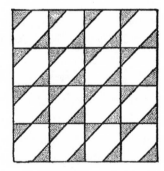

Pearly Whites

One Sunday our newspaper was delivered with a sample packet of toothpaste. I am perfectly happy with my regular toothpaste, but this was a gift, absolutely free, and therefore I kept it.

We are expecting a house guest, and I have been cleaning. I vacuumed and dusted and then turned my attention to the bathroom. I scrubbed the porcelain and polished the chrome, but the grout was still tinged mossy gray.

I remembered that toothpaste. Why not try it on bathroom tile? I found an old toothbrush and set to work. The results were amazing. If I were to take someone on a tour of the house, I would probably start with the bathroom and show off my sparkling shower. Toothpaste! Who'd have thought?

The Household Hints column in the newspaper is filled with suggestions for using everyday commodities for odd applications. Who discovered these innovations? What sort of creative people realize that ordinary things are wonder products? Quilters, especially, are notorious for solving problems in nonprescribed ways. Inventiveness is what quilting has always been about. Early American quilters pieced their quilts from scraps and salvaged worn quilts by covering them with new patchwork. They marked quilting lines by drawing

- - - - -

around dishes or rubbing soot from the kerosene lamp through little holes they'd poked through paper patterns onto their quilt tops.

Who pricked her finger and realized that meat tenderizer would remove the blood spots from her quilt?

How did someone know that hair spray would remove ballpoint pen marks?

Who first used masking tape to mark straight quilting lines? And who discovered that plain old rubbing alcohol will remove the crusty residue left by the tape? Alcohol, water, and a dab of dishwashing soap make a magic mixture that removes pencil marks from quilts. What genius put that together?

Who discovered that we can press freezer paper onto fabric or cut it into sheets to feed through our computer printers and create made-to-order fabric details and labels for our quilts?

Now the point of all this is to marvel at the inventive minds of quilters. They've had lots of practice making geometric pieces fit together neatly. They have coped with crises: spilled coffee, nicked fingers, bleeding fabric dyes, and fabric shortages. They reach into their everyday cupboards and drawers to solve problems and create wonders. They blot with paper towel, tea-dip their bits and pieces of material, and salvage the very best kind of pins from the collars of men's new shirts. They remove lint from their sewing machine feed dogs with clean mascara brushes and pull bits of thread from ripped seams with surgical tweezers.

Years ago, quilters devised quilt frames that hung from the ceiling, lowering them on pulleys to quilt during the day and raising them out of the way at night. Today we work on frames made of plumbing pipes. Surely that invention was born in the astute brain of a quilter.

Every seam we sew, every joining, every stitch requires us to be clever, to manipulate our fabric into perfect geometries, to fashion our thoughts into visible form. We turn disasters into creative triumphs. Hooray for the quilter who figured out how to piece the needle-thin points of a Mariner's Compass by stitching her fabric to paper patterns. Bless the quilter who devised quick half-square triangles. We are inventors.

My toothpaste is now tucked into a drawer in my workroom, just in case. One day I just might discover a use for it in my quilting.

Chapter 4

THE HOUSE THAT QUILTS BUILT

Flight of Fancy

Children find our stairway intriguing. Our house was built before the Second World War, and the staircase is perhaps slightly wider than those in contemporary houses. It has an open railing partially down one side that curves into the living room. The thirty-year-old carpeting covers the entire step area from top to bottom and stretches across the lower hall to the entryway. The carpet is an aged, lackluster, gold color, and it has a thick nap. I frequently vacuum up crumbs and wash out spots from where they have fallen when Bill carries his coffee and cookies up to his computer. It is, I think, not a very unusual stairway.

Yet, every four-year-old child who comes into our house (our own children, our grandchildren, and our friends' children) climbs to the top of the steps, turns, and whooshes head first, on his or her stomach, down those stairs. I clearly remember one friend's child who did a swan dive toward us, bobbled past, and smiled a beautiful smile. "Look, Mommy," she said, "I didn't even kill myself."

What is there about those steps that invites children to plunge down heedlessly? Is there comfort in the shabby warmth of the color and the depth of the pile carpet? Are they lured by the width of the steps curving into our sun-filled hallway? Do they feel a thrill from the challenge of hurtling down, or do they feel secure because they are in a comfortable environment? Why do children throw themselves down our stairs?

It is an intriguing thought, to analyze attractions and compulsions. Why do we do the things we do? Why, for instance, do we buy fabric? Rarely is the reason because we need it. We already have piles of fabric for quiltmaking. Do we buy fabric because it is comforting? Do we buy fabric because we love the color? Why do we make quilts when we could just as easily buy a commercial blanket or a picture for our walls in any department store? Certainly, a store-bought item is less expensive and would give us instant gratification.

Why do we choose to applique or to piece or to machine quilt, or to manipulate computers to produce designs with shapes and lines and shadows? Why do we play with colors and geometries when we could be using our time for practical things like washing and ironing? Why do we buy quilt books and magazines and store them in stacks in our workrooms? The libraries are filled with reading material on home decorating, gardening, cooking, technology, and quilts. Why do we store up more quilt literature than we can read in our lifetimes, and still we collect more? Why do we, who are mostly normal people, lose ourselves utterly and completely in our quiltmaking? Why?

- - - - -

I have watched children swoosh down our stairway for thirty years because they were challenged to do something exciting and daring, and in the softness of the sunlight and the carpeting, they feel secure and comfortable. Do we make quilts because of the challenge and the security?

Whether we are enticed, as children, by a sunny flight of stairs to swoosh down, or as adults, by this thing we call quiltmaking, there is a charm in it. It is a glorious thing to yield to the lure, to the siren song, to give ourselves up to the pure delight of it. Some things in life are simply meant to be enjoyed.

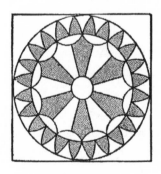 

The High-Powered Finisher-Upper

Some time ago, when Bill and I were starting out in business for ourselves, we cut our personal budget to the bone and impatiently waited out the slow times. To entertain ourselves inexpensively, we spent some of our weekends visiting real estate time-share deals. We visited sites of luxurious condominiums and country clubs, and we toured wooded areas beside streams where plots for small cabins or trailers were laid out among the trees.

Salesmen swarmed around these places. We were always greeted warmly and then given a tour of the facilities. When we came back from our tour, we were isolated in a small cubicle where we were subjected to The Hard Sell. We were offered grand inducements to buy into their plan. The whole affair was a wonderfully choreographed routine. We became quite expert, though, at saying, "No, thank you." At this point in the process, the salesman would then say that he was sure that perhaps some sort of special agreement could be reached, and that he would talk to his supervisor to see if they could "sweeten the deal." In would come The High-Powered Finisher-Upper. He would be a fast-talking, slick young man who would attempt to beguile us with fancy offers. He had the roughness, drive, charm, and persistence to bring the whole affair to a rousing conclusion.

- - - - -

My husband, Bill, however, is not a Finisher-Upper. He washes the cleanest dishes I have ever seen, but, rather than following through and putting them away, he leaves the scrubbed crockery on the kitchen counter. He puts the house to bed at night, but leaves a light still burning in his office. When he eats the last of the veggies in our serving bowl at supper, there are always a few peas left behind.

Two of my four daughters are like my husband and never quite get to the point of taking the last stitch, never binding off the incomplete elements of their lives. One patiently explained to me once that she loves having a stash of delectable works-in-progress to choose from as her mood moves her. To this day, she lives in the midst of ragged edges and turmoil, but carefully stashes her works-in-progress in remote, hidden crannies so that she can take them out some day when she is older and wiser, and she can stitch on them in the long, empty, golden moments, maybe.

The other two daughters and I are of the other persuasion; we are Finisher-Uppers. We finish things, one at a time. My rationale is that if I am doing two things, it will take me twice as long to finish them both. I love to hold my quilts in my hands, bound off, soft, clean, and done. I find the moment of completion is exhilarating. The wonder of it is that we all lived in the same house all those years, mostly in harmony.

I think these same distinctions apply to quilters, too. There are the Are-Finisher-Uppers and the Are-Nots. Some quilters pile their half-done pieces in the cupboard for a rainy day or give away their not-quite-complete blocks at guild auctions. Those are the people who take pride in enumerating their unfinished things. They are gleeful about accumulating patterns that they may make, someday, and rejoice in tops that are complete but for the want of one more fabric, or quilts that need to be bound off. This is a source of amazement to those of us who are HPFUs. The idea of having all those incomplete projects is intimidating. They would nag at us. They would dominate our thoughts and take over our lives, demanding to be finished and put away. It is amazing that these Are-Nots and the HPFUs can exist together in the same quilt guild.

But happily co-exist they do. The world must thank the Unfinishers for all of the incomplete quilt tops found in attics and at garage sales. These savers, sorters, and stashers who put their unfinished projects safely into trunks and cubbyholes have created a resource for quilt historians and an inspiration for neophyte quilters. On the other hand, as one of the great Finishers, I do not stow away my half-done bits and scruffy pieces. Instead, the best moment of all for me is when I hold my completed work in my hands, pull out the basting, and snip off the last thread ends. Only then am I ready to begin my next quilt.

- - - - -

Trash Collection

It's a glorious morning, and I am having a wonderful time. I seem to be cleaning the basement. To look at me, you would never think that I am appliqueing flowers on my wall hanging. Actually, I am appliquéing while I am cleaning the basement.

Let me take you back to the beginning of the story. I was sitting on the couch this morning, sewing what seemed like a million chintz morning glories, stitching around and around, turning under ravelly edges with my tiny needle, threading and rethreading, clipping and knotting.

My husband, Bill, interrupted my concentration.

"What shall I do with this extra microwave'" he wanted to know.

We are now the proud owners of two microwaves, one of which was a fantastic bargain at a garage sale—too good to pass up. We figured that we would store it to be used the next time our kitchen microwave died, and I was faced with the prospect of having to devote more time to meal preparation than to quilting.

"Put it in the basement." I said.

"Good heavens, where in the basement?"

I put down my needle, pulled myself off the couch, sighed, and trotted down the basement steps.

Our basement has to be seen to be believed, though

- - - - -

I suspect that there are many of you out there who can say the same. We moved into this house thirty years ago. In thirty years. I have saved everything, including all our old life jackets in case our grandchildren or great-grandchildren might go boating and need them. I have saved piles of cardboard boxes, graduated in sizes, in case we might need them for mailing.

There are boxes of upholstery fabric from the time when we all read how-to books and discovered that it was cheaper to repair the furniture ourselves. In the fruit cellar, I have saved a collection of plastic ice cream buckets, margarine tubs, and super-large frosting pails that we have scavenged from the bakery so that we could carry spaghetti sauce for high school dinners. There are plastic vases in case we ever need to take flowers to someone in the hospital and milk jugs to hold the apple juice from the annual family cidering bee.

There are chipped canning jars and all our old silverware and dishes saved to be used at someone's lake cottage, too, and under it all is a broken stool. It was broken when we bought it. That's why we bought it. It was cheap. It never got repaired. For some twenty years, anyone who sat on that stool at the kitchen counter fell off.

Suddenly, the world was like a Grade B movie. All that junk crowded in on me, stifling me, and I had a vision. It was that nobody would ever come and take that stuff away, and it would be there, filling, cramming my basement forever. Bill and I are junk collectors, and the kids occasionally add to the collection because they have no more room in their own basements, and now we are engulfed by trash.

It was at that moment I began to clean the basement. I went directly up the stairs and out the back door with an armload of cardboard boxes. I did not look back.

I took two pine-cone Christmas wreaths to my next door neighbor for a garage sale. Then, I sat down and appliquéd a morning glory.

I steeled myself for another trip to the basement. Up came a set of *National Geographics*. Why would anyone ever need two sets of *National Geographics*? I appliquéd a morning glory.

When I am finished with this flower, I will take out the broken stool. Then, I will appliqué a morning glory.

Somewhere between morning glories, I will jettison all that flotsam. I will, of course, save the prom dresses and the favorite books, and Grandma's tiny century-old Japanese tea cups. There will be a space over in the corner behind the dusty bookcases for the extra microwave. All the other corners that I am emptying will fill up again soon enough. Since the closets and shelves in my workroom are bursting with my quilting debris, I can get more of those wonderful plastic bins at the discount store, and I can work out some sort of storage pattern for my quilt stuff across one end of that empty space down there. I could put in good light, maybe a table . . . .

Another morning glory! Another dream! I simply cannot understand why some people hate to clean the basement.

To Err Is Human

When our family was younger, we had a great time making our own holiday cards. Everyone participated, and our cards were made with love and sent to special friends. Each year we made Santa puppets or patchwork shapes, and once we mailed out a mobile with paper angels.

We most often used block printing to make the cards. One year, my youngest daughter Faith was assigned the job of cutting the linoleum. She drew angels and added the word "JOY" across the top, and then dug out the unwanted areas of the design with a sharp chisel. Tired and not as cautious as she should have been, the tool slipped, and we made a fast trip to the emergency room to have her hand sewn together again. That year, no card went out for the holidays.

As February approached and Faith's hand healed, we decided to bring our distant friends up-to-date on our family activities. Faith finished cutting the linoleum, and she inked it to press it onto the top of a letter that we had written. We discovered that she had forgotten to reverse the image of her design. The angels flew gently across the paper beneath a large "YOJ." We thought it was hysterically funny and mailed our February letters embellished exactly that way. All these years later, when we get together for the holidays, we still laugh about our YOJ card.

- - - - -

When I make a quilt, I make mistakes, and I try very hard to fix them. I am a ripper virtuoso, a talented restitcher. I am a master of appliqueing clever little details over careless snips and cuts. I remember how I once deftly touched the edges of an impressive accidental slash with a fine needle that I had dipped in fabric glue. When the delicate line of glue had dried and sealed over the soft cut ends of the fibers, I pulled the edges neatly together, and then signed my name over the mended damage. My name covered the mutilation beautifully. It was an unusual place to sign a quilt, but it was neat.

It takes courage and humility to swallow my pride and confess my clumsiness, but it's a great deal of fun to devise a way to camouflage a glitch, and perhaps I will make the quilt even better. It requires spontaneity and inventiveness. And a sense of humor helps.

I have always wondered if the best quilts, the best paintings, and the best art are the result of having to recover from disasters. When my quilts turn out exactly as I plan them, perfect points, straight, smooth edges, exact in every way, they no longer feel lighthearted and exciting. Instead there is a rigidity about them. Improvisation creates variety. Little differences catch the eye. They create wonderment and stir a bit of excitement. They are satisfying. I am a great ripper, restitcher, appliquer, and camouflager, and I tell you this: no one else has any idea of the panic I feel when I have to devise some creative damage control. Being a klutz is not an easy life, but it opens your eyes and surprises you to discover how resourceful you can be. I don't know if confessing this makes me a better person, but I do think that owning up to it somehow makes for better quilts.

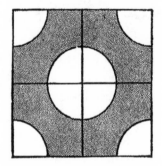

Little Drops of Water

I am a detail person. I was raised on that old poem about little drops of water making a mighty ocean and grains of sand making a pleasant land. I am intrigued with the little things in life.

Being a detail person, however, is a trap.

Many years ago, my mother-in-law asked me to make a block for her to give to someone she knew for a friendship quilt. My father-in-law decided that the quilt square should have a picture of the family's antique cider press on it, something that he felt was near and dear to them all. He made a drawing for me to follow. Being an engineer, he carefully included all of the hardware and all manner of technical parts. This precision was important to him.

I translated this drawing into the quilt block as best I could, using fabric that looked like wood and a bit of embroidery in a few key places. His disappointment was evident when I showed him the block because I hadn't included every one of the nuts and bolts and screws and cogs that was in his original rendering. I explained that it was not possible for me to include all of the tiny details as he had drawn them. In the limited space I had, and given my capabilities at the time, I couldn't put the slots on the heads of the screws or the threads around their tiny stems. It was simply not possible to include all of his minute details.

He didn't understand. He was sad.

On my latest quilt, I am making a forest. I wanted to show lots of pine trees on it, all laden with billows of snow. I struggled with those trees, and nothing that I did made them look the way I wanted. They were sadly deficient. They lacked the pizzazz that a lovely forest should have. I cut. I shaped. I appliqued. I embroidered. And I ripped out all of it.

Then the obvious occurred to me. I was trying to make pine needles and snowflakes. Instead, what I should have been making was the depth of the woods. My forest should be a mass of trees, not needles, and they should be blanketed with billows of white, not flakes.

What I was doing was laborious and distracting.

I was allowing the details to overwhelm what I was trying to accomplish.

My embroidery skills are not elaborate. Mostly I sew an outline stitch; when necessary, I make one or two french knots. The solution to my problem, I decided, was to applique a mass of green for my forest and then outline sketchy trees with white thread, just enough to give the feeling of snow-covered shapes. Now my forest is beginning to happen. The outlines of trees bent with moonlit snow are emerging, and I love what I am doing.

Detail work can become an obsession. I wanted to create the impression of trees on a cold, frosty night, but in my original version, I could not see the forest for the trees. Now the clutter is gone, and the shapes and shadows are clear and unconfused. This quilt, I believe, is far better than my original design.

I am a detail person, and I originally pictured this forest with too narrow a focus. What I've learned from this quilt is that if I can step back and simplify, I can achieve freshness in my quilting, a clarity and subtlety. I have discovered that if I can shake loose from a plan and put aside my preconceived images, I may find a new direction. Sometimes something wonderful happens with the least amount of planning.

Memories Are Made of This

A long time ago, in 1945, my brother came home. Liberated at the end of World War II from a German prison camp, he was gaunt and emotionally drained. We sat together in his room each day that summer, and he talked quietly. I recorded his memories, first with pencil and paper, and later I typed them on a rickety, portable typewriter. Bound in a cardboard cover, his memoir is a family treasure. It traces hardship and starvation and survival. A couple of years ago, I wandered around Munich talking with the warm, pleasant people and absorbing the city's Old World charm. Upon returning home, I took out my brother's journal and reread his description of that city in harsher times. I found it comforting to see how Munich has recovered from the anger and destruction of war.

Last year, Bill and I spent a day in Washington, D.C., walking through the various war memorials, reading the names inscribed on the plaques. At one of the computer kiosks by the World War II memorial, we entered my brother's name to access his war records. To our sadness, the computer replied that many Army records between 1915 and 1958 were destroyed in a fire. Nothing chronicles the service of these brave men and women. They are anonymous, but my brother is not. We have his real-life experiences on paper between two cardboard covers, a priceless journal.

- - - - -

Memories are important and give us connections to the past. I know this, but documenting hours or fabrics doesn't excite me. There simply isn't enough time to do everything. I already have another quilt in my head, and so I make excuses. I rationalize that nobody is interested. But people are interested. They want to know your inspirations, your challenges and solutions, the major influences of the time. People want a record of who you are and why you made these quilts that express your love or commemorate special celebrations. They want to remember.

I'm not a recordkeeper, but I don't want to be anonymous. I want my grandchildren to remember that every stitch I put into their quilts was done with love. So, when the quilt is all bordered, finished, bound off, and blocked, I heave a long and grateful sigh. I sit in front of the TV on a quiet, pleasant evening and watch "Masterpiece Theater" and embroider my name and the date. It takes only a few moments, and then I won't be anonymous.

The Minneapolis Institute of Art has a meticulously pieced little blue and white star quilt in its collection. There is an aura about it of gentleness, of sweetness. On the outer border, embroidered in perfect stitches are these words: Minnie A Reber/l934–35/66,300 stitches. This quilt is a testament to the loving work of Minnie Reber, who recorded her triumph by signing her name.

- - - - -

She chose not to be forgotten. We have her quilt, and we know her name. Because of this, she has become a part of our own quilting story. Hooray for Minnie Reber, who sewed a lovely quilt with 66,300 immaculate stitches! She is not anonymous, and because I sign my name, I am not anonymous, either.

Like a Bolt Out of the Blue

When a flash of lightning lights up the windows, I automatically reach over, turn off the computer, and pull the plug from the wall outlet. I am not really computer-literate. I understand only enough to handle my email. I am, however, lightning-literate. I know that when lightning speaks, I listen. I am aware that lightning can do amazing things to electrical equipment, and that it can melt down my computer innards. When lightning lashes and twitters through the sky, sometimes it seems near enough to jar my soul; sometimes I count the seconds to see how close it has struck.

Lightning is like quilting inspiration. I pay attention to that too, because I am also inspiration-literate. Sometimes the inspirations strike in strange places and at odd times, and I stop instantly to capture the sudden illumination as my own personal power surge. Sometimes I wake in the middle of the night when inspiration strikes. The impulse is so powerful it jars me awake with a flash that sorts out problems in my quilting such as what color I need to make a dark sky glow or how I should quilt my tree so it looks like it is bending into the wind. Sometimes it strikes at concerts or in committee meetings, and then I rummage through my purse and sketch my thoughts on program booklets or checkbook deposit slips. Inspiration is as instant and as flighty as a flash of lightning, and if I don't capture it right at the moment, it will disappear forever, teasing me with only fragments of the illumination lodged in my mind. When inspiration strikes, I pay close attention.

I came down at two o'clock this morning to dig through my fabric stash. Before I went to bed last night, I had been wrestling with a maroon-colored reflection in the picture of a quiet sea. Last night's fabrics were wrong! wrong! wrong! and I went to bed with the problem niggling at me. And then I had a dream. I woke suddenly, knowing that I needed the shimmer of a purple red and not an orange red, to float on that water. At two in the morning, as I laid different fabrics out upon that silent sea, my reflection suddenly came to life.

One of the lovely things about getting older is that I can indulge myself. My time is my own because I no longer have to tote children, wash their clothes, feed their stomachs, and nourish their souls; I can make or break my own schedule. I have the freedom to play with my moments. I can take the time to sort through my ideas, finger my fabrics, sketch and snip and stitch it all together, and I am at liberty to do it whenever and wherever the lightning strikes me.

A Little Squirrely

Our neighborhood has a fair number of squirrels racing across rooftops and clambering up the trunk of our great black walnut tree behind our house. Actually, that tree was planted by one of their ancestors many years ago when an itinerant squirrel broke into our garage and stole nuts from a sack that my father-in-law had brought us as a gift. The creature planted one neatly in our garden, and it sprouted and grew.

When the tree was fairly new, the neighborhood squirrels would dash up the trunk, gambol through the branches, and bite off the young nuts. Then they raced down again to retrieve them and bury them in the lawn. Since the nuts rarely had a chance to mature on the tree, I bought Bill one of those water cannon toys. When I spotted an errant squirrel heading for the tree, I would shout and Bill would race out the back door with his water gun. The squirrels laughed at us, and we had great fun. Now that the tree is older, the nuts are so plentiful in the fall that we can gather baskets full of them and still share some with the animals.

This morning I watched a remarkable display out of my workroom window. There was a squirrel who looked like a break-dancer hurtling himself through the back garden. He raced up the tree trunk out onto a sprig about three feet from the ground and flipped over

- - - - -

backwards as it bent under his weight. He dropped to the compost pile and waltzed through the finely sifted rich material, dipping into it here and there, throwing up bits of soil and leaves. Since a high percentage of the compost content is coffee grounds, I wondered if the caffeine was getting to him.

Up the tree he went again, flipping off the twig, and over and on and on with his dance without a moment's pause. I was fascinated.

As I watched, I had a sudden revelation: I saw myself. I dance too. I had been making my breakfast when a burst of inspiration flashed through my head. I saw a vision of my next quilt. I set down my cereal bowl, threw open my fabric cupboard doors, and began sifting through the reds and roses piled inside. I pulled out all sorts of possibilities. I stacked them on the floor. I fingered through blues and greens. I spilled more on the floor. I shuffled through them. I laid out paper and pencil and sketched. I pulled books off my shelf and hunted for appropriate pictures in my big file drawer. Then back to the fabric piles I went. I was excited.

This happens to me frequently. When my mind seizes an idea, I am overcome with such fervor that Bill hides upstairs in his office. To put it quite simply, I get excited about quilts. When inspiration hits, I abandon ordinary things and become lost in the creation of my dream. What looks to others like frantic activity and fancy footwork is actually merely the manifestation of all that excitement.

Do you suppose that I look like that excited, crazy squirrel to the uninitiated person, the nonquilter? Would the average self-controlled, rational human being, who has no idea of the pure joy of inventing a quilt, see my activities as madness? Would that person think I had lost all common sense and equilibrium? Or would this sane and sensible person think I had gone nuts?

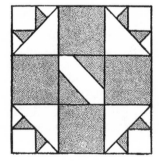

The Theory of Relativity

I've been struggling with what is supposed to be an easy definition of the theory of relativity. I understood none of it. Nada.

I asked Bill to explain it to me, and he did, sort of. Apparently, the theory of relativity has to do with time and motion and mass and how the combination relates to us. Well, it doesn't take a Mrs. Einstein to realize my relativity is all out of whack.

Let's take the first element in the equation: time. It takes time to make a quilt. This is obvious. Some people make quilts in less time than others. Some people claim to be able to make a quilt in a day, though I seriously doubt this. As for me, when I am seized with inspiration, I sit myself down and plan a quilt. If the quilt is for a special occasion, time is of the essence, and I get at my stitching expeditiously. Birthdays and anniversaries are fairly simple to deal with because if I don't work fast enough, I can always finish the quilt for next year's celebration. A quilt for a new baby is a different problem because a baby remains "new" very briefly. I have heard of quiltmakers who began quilts for a new baby, but time got away from them. They stitched and stitched and finally had the quilt finished in time for the baby's college graduation. Somehow, time is a less than reliable element, and no matter how carefully I plan, holidays, trips, and bad colds always seem to delay my finishing date.

The second element in the equation is motion. I happen to be a hands-on kind of person. Admittedly, I have a lovely sewing machine to make my life easier, but it doesn't replace the feeling of satisfaction I get when my needle takes tiny, precise stitches as it pokes through the fabric. Applique is a case in point. While the rest of the world is busy fusing and zigzagging; I tuck and shape and fasten my applique patches in place slowly and carefully by hand. This takes a lot of motion. I am a hand quilter, too. Other quilters around me sit at their sewing machines and swirl and stipple their quilts, creating three-dimensional stars and squiggles electronically. They outline and feather fast and furiously while their machines bobble up and down. I sit quietly at my quilt frame, running my needle through the layers of fabric, three stitches at a time. I prick my fingers and bend my back, but I like the gentle motion of hand quilting. I like the way it looks, puffing up gently. I like to sit and think as I hand quilt, but the motion takes much more of that first element—time.

So, I use time and motion to produce the third element, which is mass. And somehow, because my relativity is all out of whack, I seem to be spending more and more time and motion to produce more and bigger masses—quilts—requiring more and more time and motion. Do you see the tangled web I have woven?

New babies are born into my family faster than I can produce quilts. Birthdays and anniversaries and graduations are piling up on me. Holidays and special occasions fill my calendar. Always, my first thought for every one of these affairs is that I must celebrate it. Quilts! Quilts! Quilts! My days are filled with plans to make quilts. I make files of pictures and ideas for quilts. I stash fabric for quilts. I lie awake nights figuring measurements and designs for quilts, and when I fall asleep, I dream of quilts. I have more family than I can catch up with, and so far all this relativity is out of control. I have yet to figure out the equation. Given all the time and the motion involved, how can I ever produce this mass?

The Ups and Downs of Life

A while ago, I helped my daughter move. Her family has come back from Kansas, and they had a brief sojourn in a rented fourth-floor apartment until "the big things" could come up on the truck. I had thought the activity of moving would be good for me, something more physical than quilting—a change of scenery, a change of pace, a change of thought. I had been pretty swallowed up by my quilting lately.

The new house is high on a hill. I told her that she is lucky. She'll be high and dry from October until April because the snow will all roll down to the bottom of the hill! She is a smart girl. She didn't buy that. Anyhow, I arrived at the new house before the truck did. I've done a lot of moving in my life, and I thought I knew the ropes. But when that truck arrived, those boxed-up things looked enormous. The furniture is all heavy and dark like you might find on a ranch—maybe made out of an entire giant oak tree.

The movers were wonderful, nothing scratched. And they cheerfully placed everything exactly where we wanted it. It all sounds so simple, but how do you plug in an alarm clock behind a heavy dresser with the mirror mounted on top? You move it. How do you string an electric blanket cord around, behind, and under the bed, and between the mattresses? You move the bed. What do you do with the microwave when you discover that in the designated corner, the only way you can put the coffee cup inside is to reach around and over the top of the door? You move the microwave. With all this distraction, this physical activity, this change of direction, I should have been releasing all of the pent-up quilting emotion I had been harboring these last few months. This was supposed to be a catharsis.

We went to the old, rented apartment. Carrying a vacuum down four flights of steps is no big deal. But, climbing four flights of steps to get the vacuum and carry it down is a big deal. I also climbed up four flights of steps to get the laundry basket filled with linens and up four flights to get the box of books and up and up and up. As I plodded up and around and up and around and up and around, the thought occurred to me that it was just like walking up the edges of the blocks of an entire Log Cabin quilt.

When I got home, I sat in the car, limp. My husband came out to the curb to meet me. He said that we should go out to dinner at the new buffet in the shopping center. We went. We stood in line. I was so feeble that I almost got my sleeve in the salad dressing. I scattered peas in the corn bin. It wasn't until I had eaten three baked cod fillets and a dish of frozen custard that I began to revive.

- - - - -

Back home again, I felt better. I thought what a good day it had been. It was refreshing to get away from my routine. It was a joy to help my daughter settle into the house in that lovely spot. If you look down from the living room window, the street curves right around the house and on beside the lake just like a Drunkard's Trail quilt.

The hairy woodpeckers on the feeder outside of the dinette window looked like Doves in the Window. I would, of course, have to go to the car wash to remove the traces of Wild Geese Flying. Now that I had had my breath of fresh air, living a day in the life of a non-quilter like those who face each day reading books, watching TV, knitting, or jogging, I could see the world with a new perspective. I was renewed, restored. Now I anticipated the pleasure of calling my granddaughter and telling her that I would spend the promised weekend with her, helping her learn to quilt. That Little House on the Hill will be a fine place to do it. From high up there, this Prairie Queen can look down on the Wonder of the World, and late at night, she can discover what it's like to see The Moon Coming Over *Their* Mountain. So much for my day of getting completely away from quilting!

Sunshine and Shadows

There is a strange and wonderful silence in the house today. Yesterday, the Nebraska family was here, and they filled every corner with excitement. It was a joyful moment in time. There seemed to be bodies everywhere. There were people sitting and lying about, playing and eating. Plastic construction blocks covered the living room. A 1,000-piece jigsaw puzzle was spread on a table. Pillows littered the floor in front of the TV. The kitchen wastebasket was filled with empty pizza boxes, and in the upstairs hall, it was important to walk a careful, circuitous path to the bathroom, skirting the large aquarium installed there with a sun lamp that warmed Polka Dot, the Pakistani lizard. The lizard is a colorist's dream, dozing there, covered with glorious, fluorescent orange and gold spots.

Today they all went home, driving south into the winter morning. The house is quiet. This, too, is a joyful moment in time.

For a week, I gave every waking moment to them. I cooked, amused, and cleaned. I washed laundry, looked for lost treasures, and watched cartoons on TV with them, and enjoyed every moment of it. There were dirty dishes everywhere, and there were sleeping bags in my workroom, pillows and quilts behind the chair in the living room, and assorted suitcases in the basement bedroom.

Now I am standing in my quiet workroom, empty of everything non-quilt related. It is mine again, and I am gazing at the quilt that I have begun.

My current project is a small one. It is a picture of a house, and there is something strangely wrong with it. I have it laid out on the floor of my workroom, and I go in periodically and stare at it. On the left side are two large, dense trees in heavy, dark colors. On the right side there is an open area of lawn and sky with a single tree and a smaller tree toward the back. I have been troubled by the imbalance of this picture. Somehow, it seems that I must add more heaviness to the open side to match the opposite, dense trees, or else I must find a way to lighten those solid, leafy trees on the left side. The lightness of the one side and darkness of the other don't match.

Now, as the quilt lies on the floor in this quiet, I can walk around it and study it from all sides. I've cut out paper trees and placed them on the surface of the quilt. I move them around to see if adding more visual weight to one side will resolve the problem. I am obsessed with this quandary, and it is certain to keep me awake at night, tossing and turning, if I don't come up with an answer. This morning, now, in the quietness of this empty house, I am taking this uncluttered time to study the picture.

As I stand here, looking, the lightness of the lawn and sky has taken on a quality of its own. Like Lady

Justice with the scales held out before her, the balance in the picture has righted itself in my mind. Now I realize that the light is as important as the darkness. I see that if I add more foliage, the darkness will make the picture so heavy that it will disappear into dimness. If I take away some of the heavy leaves, it will be overwhelmed with too much light. It will lose some of its focal point. The sunshine illuminates the shadows. They need each other.

Sunshine and Shadows is an old quilt pattern. The light and dark pieces form larger and larger diamonds on the surface of the quilt, and without the strong contrast, the diamonds blend together, and they lose their definition. Life's like that, I guess, with joy and sorrow, hot and cold, black and white. Every element needs its opposite so you can enjoy the advantages of each of them.

This house exists in a comfortable balance of noise and silence, sunshine and shadow. I quilt in quietness when I need solitude, and sometimes I quilt in tune with the friendly beat of music on the radio. Sometimes I quilt with the tree leaves outside shading my workroom from the relentless sun, and in winter, I work with frost crystals etching my window. I quilt when I am cheerful, and quilting always rescues me from the depths of the doldrums and makes me happy. So, I will applique my picture with some shade and some lightness to make it seem as real as the contrasts in my life. Contrasts illuminate the best parts of every moment.

 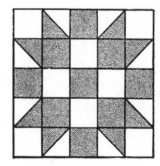

Chapter 5

I'D RATHER BE QUILTING

Out of Order

I broke myself. I always wondered if athletics and physical activity are really good for the body since I know so many young people who have had arthroscopic surgery to repair their knees or shoulders following basketball or skiing accidents. But when my doctor recommended that I walk for my exercise to tame my elevated blood pressure and raging triglycerides, I could only nod my head in humble agreement.

This morning I repositioned the quilt in my frame so that I could reach the center more easily. I set out my gold quilting thread, my scissors, my thimble, and my needles. Then I put on my warm coat, my hat, and gloves, and off I went, to walk my prescribed mile for exercise. A cardinal sang for me as I headed out the door. The air was pleasant despite the low reading on the thermometer. I started off at a snappy pace, walking in the street since the sidewalks were crusty with ice and crackling snow. Automobile traffic was light.

About halfway around my route, I noticed that the sidewalk seemed clear of ice, so I shifted to higher ground. Had I looked closely, I would have noticed that there was an ever-so-thin skin of ice on the pavement. Of course, down I went. The whole affair was very dramatic. I picked myself up and headed for home.

- - - - -

Now my wrist looks like a sausage, and my elbow is downright cranky. My quilt frame sits in the sunshine, calling to me. The gold thread waiting on it shines lovely and rich in the sunlight. I had planned to treat myself to some quiet stitching time; instead, I am shuffling around this house with untied shoes, a throbbing left arm, and a hand that is swollen to interesting proportions.

Since I can't quilt, this may be the time for me to work my way through the pile of magazines I have been saving for months. Years ago when I broke myself the last time, I made eight star quilt tops. I rotary cut them and sewed them on my machine because I could do everything using only my right hand. Now I must think. Goodness knows, I am going to have plenty of time for creative problem solving.

One thing I can work on is a pattern for a crib quilt that I fell in love with some time ago in an issue of *Quilters Newsletter*. It has a gingham dog and calico cat made of large squares and simple triangles, each creature made of a different wonderful fabric in the tessellating design. I can certainly pull fabrics off my shelves and fumble through them with one good hand. My cutting board and rulers should be easy to handle. It will be fun to plan the piecing arrangement as the ear fabric changes against the different animal backgrounds. I can lay out the pieces on the floor. My knees and legs are whole and healthy. I can stoop and bend without trouble.

Now I am excited. I am grateful, too, for this lucky break. My cooking chores are certainly curtailed, and I cannot drive the car. This fortunate accident has given me a good excuse to be utterly lazy and irresponsible. I can work at a leisurely pace and make funny, wonderful animals for my quilt, and if I am "indisposed" for very long, maybe I'll make two.

Excuse My Dust

In the corner of the living room in my friend's house there is a small table. It has a lace cloth and it is set with an antique china toy tea set. Seated around the table in little chairs are aging, beloved teddy bears having a jolly tea party. The wood in the table gleams. The china sparkles. In fact, everything in her house gleams or sparkles. It is a very clean house.

In contrast, my house is not immaculately clean. I admit that it has dust dunes and could certainly use a bit of sprucing up, but house-cleaning takes up time when I would rather be quilting. I am not seriously threatened with being condemned by the Board of Health, but this place definitely does not gleam and sparkle.

I have learned a few things over the years about keeping this home tolerably neat and habitable. For instance, my workroom tends to collect threads and bits of masking tape on the floor. I am a hand-quilter, and I have found that if I mark my quilting pattern with ¼″ masking tape, I don't have to remove any pencil marks when I am finished. Each quilt that I make seems to leave miles of basting thread and bits of tape clinging to the carpet under my quilt frame, on my shoes, and on my clothes.

Therefore, it is important that when I finish my quilt and before I begin vacuuming, it is prudent for me to swish one of those "Magic Brushes" across the surfaces of my floor and workroom to pick up the gummy, clingy debris. I try to get it first or, otherwise, the threads and tape snippets will be sucked up into my vacuum cleaner, wind around the revolving brush, and bind it so tightly that the brush stops rotating, gets hot, and begins to smoke. This is not a good thing When my vacuum brush ceases to rotate and function, it requires a lengthy session with my seam ripper, scissors, pliers, and tweezers snipping and pulling out threads and tape so that it can once more suck up debris like it is supposed to do. Using the "Magic Brush" is preventative maintenance, not high-tech science.

Threads, tape, ravelings, and snippets mixed with assorted cracker crumbs create dust, and dust is not a pleasant thing. When I was small, my mother assigned me the task of dusting all the chair rungs in the house (probably because she hated dusting them herself). When I grew older and got married, the woman who owned the house where Bill and I rented a room gave me the job of dusting the tops of all the doors and doorways (probably because she hated dusting them, too). Now, I have a deep-rooted dislike of any kind of dust-removal. I wish I were a princess in a palace and had my very own dust-removal maids. Since I do not have Upstairs, Downstairs or Dust-Removal maids, my house had accumulated dust over a very long period of time. I manage to look away and pretend it is not there.

- - - - -

Last week, a bona fide allergist with whom I was consulting identified the reason for the headaches that I have been having. Guess what! I have an allergy to dust mites. This doctor was a kind and sensitive man, and he was quick to assure me that he knew my house is not dirty (it is), everyone has a few dust mites, and it just happens that some people, like me, cannot tolerate them. His recommendation is that I make my house sparkle and shine.

Bill and I are now in the sparkle-and-shine process. We are pulling out everything and dusting, vacuuming, and scrubbing, and I figure that if I keep at this chore, at this rate I will sparkle and shine in about two years. I'd rather be quilting.

I am removing the dust from tables, chairs, beds, closets, and book cases. I am sorting hundreds of books and wiping them clean. I am trying to wean myself from all those unnecessary, dust catching things we have accumulated across the years. For instance, this family does not need a complete collection of *Where's Waldo* books. Discarding these is an easy choice, but I am distraught over making decisions about quilting books. Putting my quilting books into the give-away box would be a dastardly deed. I need them. Just having my quilting books close-by in my bookcase is comforting.

I have been sorting my fabric, and I acknowledge that I have way too much of it and should discard some. (As I have made quilts, I have added the leftover fabric to my stash. You are, I am sure, familiar with that phenomena of the more fabric you use, the more you have.) I have begun sorting by putting my cloth into identifiable, workable categories. Some of it has gone into a pile marked "Sophisticates" and some into a pile marked "Sentimentals," and I have stuffed each pile into a great, clear plastic bag. You know that I will eventually take all of those fabrics out of their clean plastic sacks to prowl through them to find the perfect pieces that I will need for my next quilt, and while I make that quilt, my rooms will once again fill up with scatterings and tatterings.

Bill is talking about putting in a new furnace and a new filter system to clean the air of my allergy-causing dust mites. He is talking about scrubbing and boiling, but I am a practical woman. I know that more dust will accumulate and more threads and more shreds. There has to be some sort of expedient way to keep this place clean, short of giving up quilt-making and taking up house-cleaning, because today's tatters are inevitably tomorrow's dust. It has taken us years to amass this accumulation. Perhaps, with effort we can get cleaned up. Then we can begin anew and we will have another thirty-five years before we reach the saturation point again. Dust seems inevitable. Still, it would be pleasant, perhaps, to have just a few years of sparkle and shine.

- - - - -

One Giant Leaf for Mankind

The Scots have a wonderful word. The word is "pauchle" (pronounced *pockle*). "Pauchle" means to cheat, to fudge—to make it work, by golly.

For instance, imagine that you are in a quilt store, and you see a piece of fabric that is absolutely wonderful, one that you must have, only it's the end of the month and the budget is short. So you pauchle it. You take some money out of the food budget and buy your fabric and have a tuna casserole for supper instead of chops. That's what it means "to pauchle."

Since I have learned the principle of pauchling, I have been astonished to recognize how much I do it every day. When I discover that the fabric for backing my quilt is an inch too short, I pauchle it. I cut the backing in half or diagonally and insert an inch or so of material, so it looks as if I was amazingly creative and arty instead of having to admit that I made a boo-boo. I am a genius at making two dye-lots of the same fabric look as if they match. I convince people that I use thread that doesn't match (when, in fact, I have run out in the middle of the night) because I want them to notice my "decorative" stitching.

Right now, I am pauchling a border. I have a great trailing vine stencil, and I have romped down the sides of the quilt, marking it quite beautifully. Now, what to do about those corners where the vines don't meet smoothly? I found a leaf that fits quite nicely over where the two sides of the stencil come together. The vines don't match at that point, but vines bend wonderfully. I just marked in a couple of extra stems. Since this is a fantasy vine, nobody can possibly know how that vine should have wandered. It is my vine, and I can make it do what I want.

Connecting the vine at the center of the borders is another story. When I began, I decided it would be easier to choose my leaf arrangement when I got there. Gleefully, I trotted along the sides, marking leaves and stems from the corners to the middle. Suddenly, I had leaves bumping into each other, overlapping, doing all sorts of strange things.

Although my borders were all exactly the same size, none of the vines came together in the middle in the same way. The fabric had wiggled and stretched as I worked with it. So there I was, pauchling leaves in the center of my borders, trying to make them all look the same when no two of them were alike.

I have finally finished marking my leaves. They are not great, but they are all right. I think I can put this quilt in the frame now and quilt it.

The great thing about pauchling is, when you become a master of the art, you do it so well, when all the to-do is over, you look back at your work and wonder what all the fuss was about. You can't even see where the crisis occurred. Its a matter of being so good at pauchling that, if you are drawing leaves, they look as if they are exactly as you had planned them from the beginning. People will believe that you were extremely clever to have designed them in such a unique way and that you did it to perfection, without effort. Nobody but you and I ever needs to know the squeezing and the manipulating that went into making the border fit.

The leaf on my border may look insignificant and small, hardly worth noticing, but you and I know all of the pauchling that went into making it exactly right. It is for me, one giant leaf.

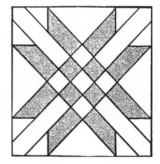

Will You Join the Dance?

I love to dance. I am a terrible dancer.

When I was a small child, my mother used to tell me that I was the only person she ever knew who could fall up the stairs. Although she sent me to dancing school to teach me grace, I never progressed past the shuffle-ball-step stage in tap dance class. In ballet, I learned to stand with my heels together, toes pointed out and hands on hips, but my bend-and-reach movement was downright awkward. My singular breakthrough came in the 1940s when I managed to accomplish a fair Low-Down-and-Dirty-Boogie.

When I grew older and more graceful (I thought), Bill and I took up folk dancing. We went to lessons every week where we twirled and sashayed, and then we changed partners. Since my other partners were, frequently, accomplished dancers, it probably wasn't a thrill for them to dance with me. My big achievement was that I learned to do an acceptable Grand March.

Today's dancing baffles me. Dancing now requires a person to make marvelous, sinuous movements, gyrating the body as if its parts were disconnected. The physical coordination that this entails is far beyond me.

I am still a terrible dancer; I am a better quilter. Why is that, do you suppose?

- - - - -

My problem with dancing can't be because I lack rhythm: "I got rhythm." I quilt in a rhythm. When my hand moves steadily across my quilt in a measured beat, I sew my straightest lines and my neatest stitches. Rhythm creates consistent work.

My nemesis can't be my agility: I am agile. Never having learned to work properly with my patterns laid out neatly in front of me on a table, I do my best work on my hands and knees on the floor. My flexibility lets me work quite comfortably down there among fabrics that are strewn around me like a glorious rainbow.

My dancing problem can't be that I am undisciplined: I am a very controlled person. To be disciplined, one makes a commitment. I am committed to my quilting to the point of compulsion. I would have no trouble staying home from a party, a dental appointment, or a grocery-shopping trip to quilt because quilting is what I do!

I have no problem with imagination: I have dreams. I picture myself as a graceful dancer. I fantasize, too, about my quilts. My quilts are born out of these lovely thoughts in my head, and then they grow beneath my fingers into textile waltzes and fandangos.

My fingers perform properly; they have the grace that is important to my quilting. Sitting quietly in my workroom in the sunshine with the sound of radio music flooding across my quilt frame, I am satisfied.

- - - - -

Fred Astaire danced to a tune that plays over and over in my memory. It went this way: "I won't dance. Can't make me!" But, my fingers are dancing while I quilt, and that's quite enough for me, thank you.

Ecclesiastes

"To every thing there is a season, and a time to every purpose under the heaven: a time to be born . . . a time to plant . . . a time to embrace . . . a time to rend, and a time to sew," and a time to give up. So says the Good Book!

It rained all night with a wind whipping against the chimney. I woke early that morning, and went downstairs to begin the work I had laid out the night before. I was going to piece ⅜″ diamonds into a Lone Star, and by adding a trunk, turn it all into a glorious little tree for my new quilt. Why? I don't know. Maybe, like the mountain climber says, "Because it is there."

Before I went to bed, I laid out all the tiny pieces, all the carefully pieced strips cut to within a thread of perfection. I had been wise enough to know that, in my enthusiasm and late-night tiredness, I was apt to sew weird lines and cut off wrong tips and pieces. "Leave it for tomorrow," I told myself, "when you are fresh."

The next morning, I came down to my workroom. It was a new day, full of promise. I was eager and excited. I stepped into a disaster. My worktable was awash. During the night, the roof had sprung a leak directly above the perfectly cut, perfectly pressed, perfectly pieced, tiny strips of diamonds. Water flowed over the edge of the table like a waterfall. Soggy diamonds floated on

- - - - -
173

the surface of the stream. I was aghast. I mopped, I dried. I pressed all those strips into wriggly, lopsided lines. Wet fabric does strange things.

I was raised in a Spartan atmosphere. My childhood upbringing taught me that, if I had a problem, I had to solve it and get on with my life. So all day long I struggled—easing, pressing, stitching, and ripping. I did not dare trim the crooked, repressed pieces. By late last night, I had indeed pieced my tree. Every point was perfect. It lay flat, sort of. Now, with judicious rotary cutting, I could trim the edges even. I had saved my tree.

I was a delusional fool! Suddenly, I faced the facts. The tree was a mess. I had struggled all day with my storm damage, and I had pieced my tree, but it was not a thing of beauty. In one swoop, I swept the star, the cuttings, the debris off my worktable and into my wastebasket. This was the time to surrender. Sometimes, giving up is winning. I found a new, better fabric. I cut it precisely, and last night, I laid it out in preparation for today's piecing. I covered it with a plastic table cloth, just in case. I went to bed.

This morning, I woke and came down to my workroom. I was eager and excited. The sun was golden in the sky. Last night's work lay waiting for me, pressed and cut. The prospect of trying to make a tree out of these lovely bits of fabric was enticing me. Yesterday is past and gone. Today is the time to get on with the rest of my life.

- - - - -

It Is Sometimes Easier to Ride a Camel through the Eye of My Needle than to Thread It

I have just had a moving experience. This day will be remembered for a long time. In fact, I may *never* forget it.

I took some very tiny, special stitches in my quilt, stood up from the frame, piled my tools on my chair, and turned the quilt once. Then, I sat down again. That's right! I sat on my pincushion.

I did not do it lightly. I was eager to get on with my quilting, and I plopped right down on the bristly thing. I rose immediately to the occasion.

I was brought up to understand that when bad things happen, you take care of them and get on with your life. I felt my backside and removed two needles. Then I cleaned off my chair, and I sat down again. I dissected the pincushion, removing not only the rest of the quilting needles I had been using, but also some others that had long ago nested deep inside it—needles that I thought had gone to needle heaven and that I would never see again.

One by one, I inspected the needles I had found. I ran them through a chunk of wool batting to oil them. I straightened them with my pliers. I stabbed them into the quilt to see if they were blunted, and I thought,

"Isn't it strange, the power of a needle?" I've heard the argument about which is mightier, the pen or the sword. My vote goes to the "mighty" needle, not because of the impression it made on me when I sat down on it, but because of the things it has helped me and others create, the variableness of its personality to be cooperative and caring or to be contrary and obtuse, and, yes, its power to hurt me or help me, as it chooses.

That slender little snippet of steel has a mind of its own. It has an eye that will or will not allow itself to be threaded. It has a point that will or will not nip through the layers of my quilt, sometimes gliding like butter, sometimes balky as an old cat that won't be moved from a sunny windowsill. It does not always stitch the straight and narrow. It may stray a bit, bend its back to the weight, develop a slightly twisted personality, and if you push it or demand too much of it, it may snap. Sometimes, that silvery sliver may be as straight and pure as a maiden in a fairy tale, dancing lightly, skipping through its days making perfect little impressions, its delights inspiring me to golden laughter. Sometimes it can be sly or coy or stubborn.

My needle is an inconstant thing. I can be sure of just two things—its vagaries and its faithfulness. It is always close when I need it (today closer than I would like to have had it), and, next to my toothbrush, perhaps the most personal tool I own.

- - - - -

When I read about the pioneer women who shared one needle, or the quilters who had needle cases they kept on their mantles to hold their single needles, I am grateful for my bounty. I can go to the store and buy needles today, tomorrow, whenever. I can keep a kit filled with needles. If I drop one in the carpet, I can vacuum without worrying that there will be no more needles. I can afford to let them slide deep into my pincushion to be discovered another time—perhaps.

I have readjusted my chair and pulled my frame a little closer to the window for better light. I have bent my needles back into shape. I have sharpened them, tested them, and readied them. I have threaded them and lined them up in pincushions ready for some really good moments of quilting. We live in a wonderful time: a copious quantity of fabric in all hues and styles, bright electric lights even into the late-night hours, leisure time to quilt, and, best of all, an abundance of needles. We are blessed!

Sinking to a New Low

When those pneumatic chairs first came on the market, I was crazy to have one. You know the kind I mean: with the touch of a lever, the chair floats up or down to whatever height pleases you.

This new convenience promised me wonderfully comfortable happy days ahead while I stitched away on each new project, whether I was hunched over my quilt frame hand quilting or sitting at my sewing machine.

I went out and priced the chairs. Being a new and modern convenience, these chairs were, of course, beyond my pocketbook. So off I went to a secondhand furniture store where I found just what I was looking for at a price I could afford. A man at the store helped load the chair into my car, and I drove home. I was in seventh heaven.

My new black and chrome chair looked stunning in my workroom. I sat in it, turned around once, and fell over. When I picked myself up off the floor and investigated, I found the chair had a wonky wheel. I should have known there was a reason it had been in a used furniture store. I took the chair back to the shop, where the salesman looked it over.

"Easily fixed," he said as he swapped the broken wheel for one from another chair in the store. At least my chair was healthy again.

- - - - -

At home, I sat in my new chair daily, stitching away cheerfully at my sewing machine. The chair was perfectly adjusted for my body, and each time I used it, I knew that I could sit and whip out intricate piecing in perfect comfort.

But a surprise awaited me. Just like a brightly colored party balloon loses its zip over time, my used chair started to lose something. As the years passed, it drifted lower and lower at an imperceptible rate, until one morning I realized I was seated considerably lower than when I first sat down. I was, in fact, so low that my eyes were almost level with my sewing machine's needle. Mighty low.

The downward drift came on so slowly that I hadn't known it was happening. I analyzed the situation. Although I ended up sitting in an unusual position, I realized this unconventional posture was a really great innovation. Now, as I sit at my machine feeding fabric under the needle, I am looking dead-on, sighting down the seam line like a sharpshooter aiming a gun. My seams are incredibly straight and accurate.

Never in this world would I tell someone else to hunker down at this peculiar height to operate a sewing machine, but I like sitting like this now. I have become accustomed to it. Strange things happen when you least expect them.

For years I've thought that tall women are gorgeous. Able to reach things at heights well over my head, they are always in demand at guild meetings to hold up quilts brought for show-and-tell. Having always wanted to be a woman with greater stature, my first impulse this morning was to ratchet my chair back up. On second thought, however, I believe I shall keep my secondhand chair where it is.

I have always known that doing patchwork was good for the soul. I've found it uplifting. I never expected, though, when sitting in my chair to make quilts, I would sink to such depths.

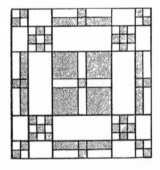 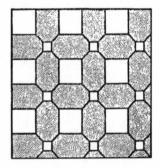

Aitch-too-oh

It has rained and rained and rained. For one week now, every day, a deluge of rain has fallen from the sky. Bill likes to stand in the window watching the monsoon as it cascades down. "It's going to get better," he says.

"That's what Noah said," I reply.

On the back table is a long list of things I plan to do when and if the sun ever comes out.

1. Plant the pansies.

2. Spray waterproofing solution on my raincoat.

3. Scrub the mud off the kitchen floor.

4. Photograph the quilt that I have just finished.

5. Take the red fabrics from my stash out into the natural sunlight so I can sort and choose the roses and the rubies for the next quilt that I am arranging on the floor.

6. Wander around the neighborhood with my camera and discover what miracles with lovely new leaves and bright blossoms have sprung from the sodden earth.

7. Air the bed quilts.

8. Celebrate.

When the sun comes out, I will open the windows and breathe in the scents of the season, the lilac fragrances and the hints of fresh-mown grass. I will stand behind the house and watch the bedraggled robins and their new families that have huddled in their drenched nests

- - - - -

built up behind the downspout by the corner of my workroom—when the sun comes out.

At this moment, another squall is shaking the window. I pull my circle of lights closer around me as I am working. A stormy day is the time for finishing things, and my stack of unfinished projects is piled on the worktable beside me. Today, I am making a friendship block for a wedding quilt, and I am tacking down the last unstitched areas on a quilt that my needlework group is making for a hospice. I shall bind off a little miniquilt that has languished on my table, nearly done, for some time. I have a collection of scraps that need sorting and folding and putting away, and when that is done, I shall vacuum up all those squiggly threads and bent pins that have strewn themselves across my workroom floor.

When the rains subsided, old Noah stood on the deck of his ship as it began to settle back onto the earth. He sent out a dove to see if it would return with a fresh, new leaf in its beak as a signal that the water was going away and life was beginning to reappear. While he looked at the sky, he saw a rainbow that promised him that the floods were indeed over. I stand here and look out of the window as the rain begins to ease. Piled beneath the panes are the rainbow colors of my projects, glowing in the gray light of the last rainstorm.

- - - - -

This has been a wet, endless spell of weather, but I am grateful because I realize that without the rain, I would be drowning in unfinished projects. In this soggy weather, raindrop by raindrop and stitch by stitch, I am completing my bits of work and putting my life back in order. Moment by moment and project by project, I am accumulating sanity and satisfaction.

When my family was young and the children and I were shut inside the house on rainy days, I used to recite that old poem about "little drops of water making a mighty ocean," and sing songs about April showers and "Singing in the Rain," and the children would say, "Mom, you are such a Pollyanna."

I suppose I am. But once I have pulled myself out of my rainy-day funk and reconsidered all the rewards of quiet confinement, I find myself free to enjoy the promise of those rainbow colors radiating through the dullness of this wet, wonderful weather.

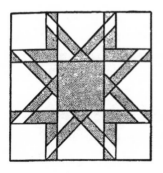 

Time Goes By

Recently on one of those news magazine programs on the television, the commentator discussed the great success of the Hubble telescope and explained why it is so important to all of us. I had always supposed that it was simply a bigger and better telescope, much like the structures on mountaintops here on earth, taking pictures of the stars. But the gist of the news story, as I understood it, was that the telescope is so deep into space that it is flying around up there in light that was emitted from the earth eons ago. We're talking about ancient light that has traveled slowly through space, being what the speed of light is, and it is only now reaching the place where the Hubble telescope is orbiting. Therefore, the pictures that the telescope is taking at this moment show the earth as it was ages ago.

With the information that they are receiving from the instrument, scientists are revising their theories concerning the earth. Where once they believed that the earth is slowing down in its rotation, now they have discovered that the earth is actually spinning faster and faster. Why didn't they ask *me*? I could have told them that.

My whole existence is spinning out of control. Spring flies by so quickly with summer tromping in on its heels that fall bursts upon me, followed almost immediately by winter roaring in. Suddenly the ice and snow are

- - - - -

melting, and spring prances in for another visit. Only this time when it comes, it is already the next year.

I cannot catch up. My quilt ideas are piling up in my head. I merely find time to scan the books that I have stacked up, when my initial intention was to study them and make notes. My fabric is accumulating at an amazing rate. If I don't buy that special material when I see it, it will be gone tomorrow. The colors and prints change so quickly on the store shelves that there seems to be a whole new lot every week. I want more and more, faster and faster, in case I ever need it.

The calendar of quilt events in my magazine overwhelms and frustrates me. I used to carefully mark items and schedule time for everything close to home. Now, there are amazing shows and classes happening everywhere, and I cannot possibly fit them all into my life. I used to amble along. Eventually I trotted. Now, I feel like a jogger breaking into a gallop, and I will never, never catch up.

As my quiltmaking gets squeezed and scrunched into smaller and smaller spaces of time, I panic. I get up early and work late at night. The minute hand on my clock spins around before my eyes. Quilting explorers and experimenters may not worry about time as they continue on, cheerfully trying new patterns and techniques. They may never finish their projects, but it doesn't matter. Their aim is to taste new things, try new ideas, and enjoy their discoveries. They are blessed with a philosophy that allows great joy in playing with their quilting.

Those of us who are finishers are in a different frame of mind. We try to quilt in double time, carrying our projects with us when we go out in case we find a spare minute in our day. Once, I worried that I might not have an idea for a new quilt; now I make fast sketches and jot down notes so that I can keep up with the flood of ideas in my mind. Now I quilt quicker and think faster and cook nearly instant meals.

The only answer to this high-speed dilemma, I have found, is to abandon my hold on reality. I take time to dream. Last night at supper, Bill suggested that we ride out into the country, so I abandoned my quilting plans for the evening and the goals I was determined to meet. Instead, we drove out into the warmth of early summer, and I escaped into the gloriousness of the red-winged blackbirds clinging to the reeds in the marshes. Egrets were standing in feathery white beauty along the shores of lakes. Along the edges of the road, the landscape was awash in the lushness of the full, green leaves. It was a moment to slow down in the race. It was a time to rest. It was a time to breathe.

Back on planet earth today, it is whirling again. My moment in that other time has given me a respite. I can cope. I will bind my quilt today, sign it, and put it away so that I can begin my next challenge. I am a newer, fresher person because I stopped for a bit and my world slowed down.

Little Things Mean a Lot

Hamlet, Prince of Denmark, said it exactly right: "There's something rotten." My car has a strange, prevailing odor, and it is most unpleasant. I've gotten on my knees and sniffed across the floor and around the back seat like a bloodhound, but I cannot for the life of me find out where that ugly smell is coming from. I have taken out every single thing that is movable, including the seats, and vacuumed it from top to bottom. I have scrubbed it with upholstery cleaner. The smell persists.

Last week I took the car to the service department at the local car dealer. "Hmmm," said the service supervisor, "it smells like a dead animal."

So, the garagemen took the car apart. They examined the engine, the cooling system, and all that mechanical confusion under the hood. They found no animal. They found no strange leaking fluids. They found nothing. The car still smells.

Tomorrow, I have an appointment with an auto detailer. If anyone can find the problem, he should be able to, I think. I have great faith in this plan, because, somehow, I feel a kinship with anyone who deals with "details."

When you stop to think about it, you and I are quilt detailers. Like it or not, when we are sewing little pieces of fabric together to make a big quilt top, we have to deal with details. It would be wonderful to throw ourselves into quiltmaking casually and haphazardly and watch the pieces simply fit together magically. But if we did, I'm afraid we would not be pleased with our results. If our quilt tops are going to go together smoothly, we have to pay attention to little things like accurate cutting and careful piecing. If we want the quilting designs to bloom on our quilt, we have to mind our stitches and our knots. In other words, we have to pay attention to the small issues, because it's those details that make our quilts so glorious.

When I finish a quilt, bind it off, and sign and date it, I lay it out on the floor of my workroom just for the pure joy of seeing it there, complete. Usually, it thrills me. Once in a while, though, a quilt will have a restless feeling about it, something that is not quite right with it.

That's exactly how I feel about this new quilt that I just spread out. I was ready to celebrate its completion, but there is something unsettling about it, something I cannot define. This quilt has delicious colors and careful piecing. It is quilted with gentle puffs and soft curves, and it is bound off with straight, even edges. Why does it seem still unfinished to me?

I left the quilt lying on the floor of my workroom, and I have gone back every once in awhile to see if I can decipher this mystery. Now, in the soft evening light I

- - - - -

see it. There is, somehow, an emptiness around the birch tree just to the right of the center. The tree is partially outlined in a deep, dark indigo fabric. The part of the tree that is not outlined is lost against the background, fading into nothingness where it should be strong and stark. Such a tiny detail, such a puny problem! Fortunately this time it is something so simple to fix.

While I am sitting in the living room this evening in the glow of the TV light, I will simply touch the tree here and there with my needle to make a few indigo-colored outline stitches, just enough to define the tree against the background and give it strength. It is such a tiny detail, and with only a few moments of work, it will satisfy my quilt. And it will satisfy me.

I am a quilt detailer. The fine points are important to me because each small touch comes from my imagination and makes this quilt my own. It would be easy to leave this quilt as it is with its gentle, vague tree standing in nothingness, but this is not what I had intended. I wanted to make a crisp, bright birch tree etched sharply against its background. In order to make this quilt be what I envisioned it to be, I need to pay attention to the details.

My Druthers

I was standing in my kitchen making hamburger pie at seven o'clock this morning. The pie is an old family favorite called Delicious Promise, from the time when the only thing I cooked for my big batch of people was something made with ground beef, unless it was hot dogs.

I am going to a quilt affair this morning, and I'll be away for several days. I always cook up something that the family loves and leave it in the refrigerator. I don't know whether it's because of guilt for leaving these big capable adults to fend for themselves, or if it's a promise that I will come back to them and cook their meals and clean their home again.

Anyway, there I was, chopping and frying and stirring. I watched the broiler carefully as I melted the thick slice of Swiss cheese into the top of the pie, waiting until the cheese bubbled up and browned at the center—just the right moment to whisk it out of the oven. It was perfect!

Cooking is something I do nowadays without a great deal of enthusiasm, unless it's this Delicious Promise sort of thing. When you consider forty-two years times 365 days times three, plus all those in-between peanut butter sandwiches, I've done a heap of cooking, right? I know there are a lot of you who have cooked as much if not more. You know what it is to wake up every morning, and think, before you even put your foot out of bed, "I wonder what I should take out of the freezer to thaw for supper."

This morning as I stood there in the center of my kitchen in the early light, I thought about the people who love to cook. As I chopped and measured, it occurred to me that at that moment I was cooking exactly in the same way I quilt. I was measuring and cutting and putting together precisely. I was considering the color, the blend, the rightness of it all. This morning I was cooking with love.

Don't get me wrong. I have not gone hog-wild over cooking. It's just that I realized when you make something with love, it takes up all of your time and attention. When I quilt it's exactly like that. I am obsessed with the feel, the blend, the precision and the wonderful way it looks when it is done. My eyes taste my quilts; they savor them.

And when I quilt, I do it with such a passion that it crowds out all the other distractions—like cooking—that vie for my attention. I don't want to bother with the regular daily things that can be put off. The laundry can be done another day. The dust will be only slightly deeper tomorrow. I quilt with love, and given my druthers of consuming passions, quilting is mine.

If you come to my house and I invite you for a meal, I will put down my needle and fold away my fabric for a while. I will stop my sewing, and I will slice and toss and trim and stir.

Or, maybe I'll just take you out to lunch.

- - - - -

Small Favors

The window shade flapped around the roller three times when it slipped out of my fingers this morning. I stood in front of the window in my nightgown and looked out into a world that was wet and gray and chilly. In the lexicon of my family, it was an "Ugl," the superlative of the word ugly: *ugly, uglier, ugliest, ugl.* An hour later, as I drove my daughter to school. I commented with a sigh, "Well, at least the wind is not blowing!"

"Neither," said she, "is there an earthquake, fire, or flood. Mom, how can you find something good in any situation?"

"Well," said I, "I suppose I am thankful for small favors."

I am a Pollyanna: this is my salvation. I tend to get caught up in the emotions of a crisis. In other words, I panic in a pinch. If I couldn't find those small favors, I'd be lost. I would fail to find any creative solution that would bail me out of the mess I was in. For instance, when I snip a hole in my quilt as I am taking it out of the frame, I am grateful that I know how to applique small flowers. When I calculate my fabric just one patchwork piece short, I am grateful for the shop-owner who dips into her hidden cache to find a quarter of a yard to match my own discontinued material. When I discovered that I couldn't match thread to my current project, my friend who is a garage sale fanatic produced a hundred salvaged spools of thread wrapped neatly on their wooden cores, a whole peacock-tail of colors. I am grateful for her, too.

Those of us who plunge whole-heartedly into our work are not inept. We are impulsive. In the excitement of creating, we do not consider our projects calmly. Our lack of forethought becomes a painful afterthought. The small favors are the blessings.

Right at this very moment, I am in need of a small favor. I have just broken my last quilting needle and the shops are all closed for the night.

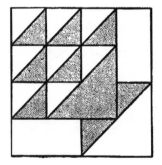

Chapter 6

THIS
PATCHWORK LIFE

Ode to a Grecian Urn

Up the road a piece is one of those places that sells the leftovers from stores that have gone out of business. It is a marvelous place to find hidden wonders at astonishing bargain prices. Occasionally, I like to browse there on treasure-hunting expeditions. On my last foray, I discovered a ceramic pitcher. It was white, and embossed on the sides were the lovely, rounded clusters of grapes touched with an imitation patina of age. It had the grace and beauty of a Grecian classic, and I fell instantly in love with it.

I do not need a new pitcher. I have shelves of crockery in my basement that I have collected for more than fifty years. Excess, Waste, and Needless Spending are cardinal sins to me since I was a "child of the thirties" and raised to be thrifty, but I had fallen in love with that pitcher.

So I made excuses to myself as to why I must have it. The pitcher was pleasantly short and squat, I told myself, and it would fit neatly in the limited space beneath the cooling unit in my refrigerator. It was the perfect size for iced tea. Besides, it was very cheap, and it would be absurd to pass up such a bargain. I bought it, and I felt extravagant and sinful.

This morning, as I was putting away the clean, dry dishes from the dish drainer, I cradled the pitcher in my hands. It felt smooth and flawless and graceful. It was beautiful, and it gave me deep-down pleasure.

I've always thought that if something is beautiful, it can only be a blessing. I feel that way about my quilts. Once when a woman asked me, "What do you do with all those quilts?" I answered her directly, and I made no excuses. I said, "I love them. I touch them. I count them. I look at them and I study the fabrics, and sometimes I sleep under them." Quilts give me pleasure.

We have a quilt on our bed, and at night, I fold the quilt back carefully to protect it because I know the hours of labor and the cost of fabric and the creativity that went into its making. It is a treasure. I try hard not to rumple it or wear it out, but I have accepted the fact that this is a sleeping-under quilt. Everything has a purpose, and the purpose of this quilt is to keep me warm and make me happy.

I made a wedding quilt for us when Bill and I were married. It has long since worn out. Bill sat on the edge of it every night to take off his shoes and socks, and gradually the edges wore thin and then shredded. I mourned the tatters that it became. Those tatters are not a shame or a disaster, though, but a testament to the moments I loved making it, looking at it, feeling it, and sleeping snugly beneath it. If it had been folded away pristinely, it would probably still be a healthy piece of needlework, but it would not have been a cherished part of my life all these years.

- - - - -

Some homes are filled with stunning art and tasteful touches. The rooms are decorated in coordinated colors and have matching furniture. Small, enchanting items are scattered about on table tops and tucked into corners. There are no worn threads or ravelly edges visible.

My own home is rather frayed. The furniture is dated. There are small coffee spots here and there on the carpet. But my bed has a quilt on it that I love. This quilt was made with loving hands with colors that stir my soul. I pull it up beneath my chin at night, and I snuggle under it. I know that some day, it will begin to show signs of wear; the simple laws of time and use tell me this. I don't mind, though, because to me it is beautiful, and I made it to be used and loved.

Having a beloved quilt, or for that matter, a Grecian pitcher, is to have a thing of beauty, and even when it is worn and old, it will be a joy forever.

- - - - -

Encore! Encore!

"My word," my husband said. "What was all that about?"

I had been standing in the shower in the rosy glow of the pink plastic curtain with the hot water shimmering off my head. As so many people do in the shower, I sang. I am not a good singer, but I belted out a red-hot-mama song. "Way Down on the Mississippi," I sang, and suddenly I realized that one of the notes swelled and mellowed each time I sang it—one note— a single full, round note. Then, I remembered one of those seemingly useless bits of information that I had learned years ago. It was about that place in time and space where a tone resounds. My voice slid up and down the scale, and as it passed over that same note again and again, that tone rang clearer and more intensified than all the others. Standing surrounded by those wet tiles and closed in by the water-beaded shower curtain, the damp air picked up that note and turned it into the rich, full tone of a virtuoso's violin. I turned off the water and wrapped a towel around my body. Still singing that single note, I ran downstairs to finger the keys on my organ to see if I could find the note. It was high C. I don't know what specific elements affect that point of resonance; tomorrow with a different water temperature, a different barometric reading, high C might not resound as beautifully as it did in my shower today, but this morning, the sound and the moment were glorious.

I experienced a moment of resonance, too, last evening, when I turned my quilt frame upside down, with its plastic feet sticking up in the air. I looked at the back side of the quilt, the one I have been working on for over a month. I wanted to study my quilting pattern to see if it filled the entire surface adequately and evenly. As I looked at it, the moment resonated like that lovely moment in my shower. All of those tiny stitches, all of the soft domes of the feathered design rose up and filled me with joy. The sweetness and the delight of it bombarded me.

Unless we are very small children, we have lived through a lot of moments to remember. Some are sad ones, some glad ones. The moments I remember best are not cataclysmic events but the little bits and pieces of time that have resonated in my mind. I have kept the echoes of them, and I take them out now and then to re-experience them. Sometimes the moment has been something I've seen, like the magic day I saw, just for a minute, a great horned owl perched high in a tree beside my house. It sat so silent and still that at first I was not even aware that I was seeing this wonder outside my kitchen window. When I looked again, the owl was gone, all gone but for the echo of it in my mind. Now, on silent, gray days, if I look up into that tree, the magic vibrates through me again.

Another time on a gentle summer night, I heard, in the dusk, a child call, "Olley, olley, outs in free." It struck that note in my heart. The miracle of a long-ago time flooded through me. I remembered a lovely twilight when I was young: In that moment the air was gentle, and I was a child again, playing hide-and-seek on a shadowy lawn.

I guess many of us are quilters because we can capture the rich moments of our work and can play back the resounding glow. Sometimes quilting is frustrating, late at night when our eyes tire and our thread knots. In the light of day, though, when we look again, we see the miracle of all of those little stitches and the repeat of the curves and dips. In that instant, the moment resonates, and the wonder of creating that quilt comes flooding through us to be replayed again. Nothing takes the place of the feeling of elation that bursts in us then and leaves little bits of sweetness echoing in our minds.

Is this the magic of quilting then? Is it a miracle that we can capture the moments of wonder and fold them away on our shelves, and every time we take down our quilts, unfold them, and spread them out, the glory of them floods through us and sings to us again?

Silver Threads

I must have looked appalled!

I met a young woman at the State Fair. She makes and sells folk costumes, and she is a fine craftswoman. I was excited to discover her meticulous detail, her sensitive use of color. We talked for a long time, and I came away aglow.

Several days later a friend told me that she had talked with the young woman at the fair, too. The two of them had discussed sewing and design and had talked about how much I had enjoyed my earlier conversation. And then the young woman had remarked about me, "She's a feisty little old lady!" The tale-carrier must have seen the shock go through my body. She hastened to assure me that this had been meant as a compliment. She said it several times.

Later, in the quiet of my own mind, I thought over her comment.

Feisty. That's not such a bad thing to be. I know that I am frequently enthusiastic. I also know that when backed into a corner, I come out fighting.

Lady. That's pretty good. Obviously she could see more in me than my jeans, my rumpled hair, and my holey tennis shoes.

But *old*? True, I am not thirty years old. In fact, I have children older than that. But I am young enough to attack life with an abundance of energy. When I prepare a quilt for the frame, I crawl around on my hands and knees, pinning, basting, trimming. I do a lot of floorsitting. I will admit that I use two bright lamps to do my appliqué, but certainly that has nothing to do with age. Everyone knows that good work requires good lighting.

I am aware that my waist is expanding, but it still fits nicely under a quilt frame. My hips look like any other quilter's hips, give or take a few pounds. When visitors come to see my Grandma Kelley quilts, they always look appropriately astonished as they come up my front walk and exclaim, "But you can't be Grandma Kelley!"

Old? I can't be old. I won't be old. Old is the twilight years when you sit and quietly rock as you stitch. (I guess I do that sometimes.) Old is when every word is wise and gentle and discreet. (I frequently have to remind myself that every word I utter is not wisdom and that I am often in danger of being a bore.) Old is having people wait on you and take care of you. (My children will certainly deny me that.) Old is wrinkles. (I have a few.) Old is that time of life when you slow to a stop, put down your quilting, and drift off into the sunset.

I am not old. I will not be old. But a feisty lady—you bet!

Sounds Good to Me

Sitting here in my workroom, I've been busy sewing my name on a quilt, and I can hear a sound. It goes plunk–plunk–plunk, and then a pause, and more plunk–plunk–plunk. I can't see anyone outside my window, I know exactly what it is making that sound. Somewhere in the neighborhood there is a high school boy dribbling a basketball and shooting hoops against a backboard mounted above his parents' garage. That sound happens on days somewhere between spring and summer when the sun is bright and the air is fresh. The plunk–plunk–plunk tells me that warmer weather will be coming along soon.

Other sounds speak to me, too. The other day, I lifted the pile of wet laundry out of my washing machine and transferred it to my dryer. I cleaned the lint trap, slammed shut the dryer door, pushed the "on" button, and in an instant I knew from the rattle–clunk–ding that something was wrong. I opened the dryer door to stop the mayhem, and I immediately grabbed the phone to call the repair service. The rattle–clunk–ding told me all I needed to know.

If we take the time to listen, we can hear messages from the world about us. Is there anything lovelier than the whir of a newly cleaned sewing machine motor, purring gently and flawlessly? It says without words that it is ready to plunge into a new, exciting project. No matter what your favorite music style, this is a sweet song to us quiltmakers.

On colder days when the sky is gray, when the weather cannot decide what the season is, I can hear twittering birds warming themselves in the chimney. They make a satisfying sound. The chirping makes me huddle closer to my quilt frame in the lamplight. The gentleness of the music on my radio murmuring in the shadows around my nighttime work table encourages me. The sound of comfortable solitude, a thoughtful quietness, surrounds me when I lay my patchwork pieces on the carpet and shuffle through them to devise patterns.

Last Friday night, when Bill and I went out to the mall for dinner, we were seated close to a tableful of deaf people. I watched them unabashedly as they talked silently to each other. They signed jokes. They exchanged news. They celebrated a birthday. All of this was done in silence. I was filled with a feeling of awe. It made me grateful. The sounds of my workroom blend. The undertones resonate around me. The laughter of my grandchildren and the hissing of my steam iron, the snip of my scissors, the ringing of my telephone, and the deep, hard sigh that says I am thinking. I hear the sounds, the plunk–plunk–plunk and the twitter of the birds, and I incorporate it all as part of my quilts.

- - - - -

Hands Off!

Bill has fixed my computer. In his past life, my husband Bill once had the official title of "control engineer." Translated into English, it means that he loves to figure out what makes electrical things work. Instead of reading the directions that come with equipment, he enjoys finding things out on his own. We have a TV-CD-DVD-tape-FM/AM radio-VCR-speaker arrangement in the living room that would be the envy of other control engineers. All of this is fastened together with an assortment of cables and switches and topped with a set of rabbit ears that dip and curtsy with the turn of several knobs. I never touch this setup. It terrifies me.

It is in Bill's nature to play with electrical equipment. My computer was fine and didn't need help, but Bill fixed it. It's a nice, simple machine, and I only ask it to send and receive email, do a bit of word processing, play an occasional game of solitaire, and once in awhile, make a foray onto the Internet. By computer standards, these are pretty simple tasks, and it was performing well. It didn't need fixing.

Last night, however, Bill said, "What do you think of this? You can have a forest or a mountain." My usual screensaver, a picture of a lovely cloud formation, was gone.

"I like my sky," I replied. "Put it back."

- - - - -

This morning when I turned on my computer, the screen was navy blue. I clicked a few buttons. My solitaire game was backed with a forest green, so dark it looked as if it were twilight in an abyss. My Internet connection was a mustard yellow.

"Put it back," I said again.

"I will," he said, which usually means, "sometime." He seemed fairly unconcerned. He had, after all, only changed the color.

But I am amazed how color affects my life. Now I only need to pass by my computer desk and I feel the angst rise in my body. I cannot play solitaire in a dark forest. I will not even attempt to go out onto the jaundiced Internet. I make very quick trips to collect my maroon-colored email.

Color does amazing things to people's hearts and minds. It can cheer us, refresh us, uplift us, make us feel safe and trusting. Never, though, have I had such a good example of the distress that color can cause. While I usually like dark colors, I cannot work among them. It's as if they smother my creativity. I see quilts that people make in dark hues of midnight blues, murky golds, deep dark reds, and purples like twilight settling in, and while I find these quilts dramatic and exciting, I could never, ever, make one. If you are someone who likes that strong palette, you will wonder what my problem is. You might be bewildered by my quilts, full of bright reds, peaches, lilacs, and yes, sky blues. My quilts might strike you as gaudy, whimpy, or unimaginative.

It would be interesting to compare the stashes of other quilters, the ones who make bright, chrome-colored quilts, the ones who use soft-dusky colors, and the ones who prefer soft, spring flower colors. I'll bet you will find as great a variety of people as you will find colors and quilts.

A La Mode

Style is a strange thing. We contort the human form in the name of fashion, and in the effort to be chic, we grow to think of modish distortion as beautiful. In the 1800s, women wore large construction projects, called panniers, that hung from their waists. Antebellum dresses were hooped out to astonishing proportions, and Victorian ladies wore birdcage-like contraptions, called bustles, to enlarge their backsides.

Some fashions that were fairly attractive or comfortable seem to make cyclical comebacks. Saddle shoes and loafers reappear periodically. Even the beehive hairdo was recycled from the enormous French hair fashions of Marie Antoinette's time. (It has been claimed that they were so big and permanently constructed that, once, a mouse was actually found in one.)

We tend to think that the best fashions are those which were in style when we ourselves were at our youngest and loveliest. I prefer dresses with flaring skirts that show tiny waists. I like pleasantly fitted bodices that display the best parts of the human body gracefully, with a bit of mystery, and that don't expose natural folds and (let's be honest) bulges.

Industry has set the style in clothing, titillating the buying public, pressuring it to want new and more. This same commercial pressure is happening with quilting, too. I find myself falling into the trap. Wonderful new fabrics flow through the quilt shops in an endless stream. I see things so delicious that I want a lot of them, right now.

I watch people looking through piles of old quilts that evoke other years, other centuries. Mostly, these people finger them, talk to them, and admire them. Recently, though, a less-discriminating acquaintance looked at one of my old treasures and asked me why I had bought "that ugly quilt." "Because it cost $35," I said. I didn't explain to her that the orange and brown pieces were interesting fabrics that meant something to me in the framework of history. She wouldn't have understood.

In one hundred years, what will people think about the quilts we are making now? Will the fabrics I use date my quilt? Should the style of my fabrics make a difference? One of the best things that has happened in the last twenty years is that people have become aware that a quilt is a creative product, and we have learned to respect the inspiration and circumstances behind the making of it. The fabrics, techniques, and designs are the quiltmaker's tools, and they have nothing to do with style.

There will always be people who buy bedding because it is modish and matches the wallpaper. But truly discerning people will preserve and cherish the quilts we are making now because quilts have moved beyond fashion's dictates. It's a wonderful thing when uniqueness moves past the limits of fashion and we celebrate creativity. With quilts, there is no prevailing taste, only a variety of choices that are limited only by the quiltmaker's preferences. When I go to the quilt store, I can buy dabs of this and that fabric if it pleases me, and I can make what I like because, with quilts, nothing and everything is in style.

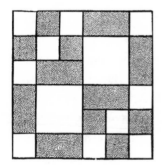

Feeling Groovy

Once upon a time, when I was young, I lived a pretend "Cinderella" life. My fairy godmother lived in midtown Manhattan, and I lived in New England. Each year for my birthday, I boarded my pumpkin railroad coach and rode into the Magic City. The train rumbled past sooty towns and green fields, then into New York where it came to a stop at the Castle (Grand Central Station). For that one whirlwind weekend with my fairy godmother, I got to do princess-type things. I went to theater matinees and the opera. I went to the Roxy Theater and then for luncheon, we stopped at Schraft's, where a string quartet fiddled Mozart melodies. On Sunday, promptly at the stroke of twelve noon, I boarded my coach and rode back to Everyday Land where I became myself again.

New York has enchanted me ever since those days. I've been back again and again, and every time I have the same feeling of excitement. Sometimes I've simply passed through on my way to Someplace Else. Other times I've dropped into the city to wander through a museum for a day. In 1986 I went back to attend the big quilt show that celebrated the renovation of the Statue of Liberty. Each time I relived my younger years.

New York had a feel about it. I remember the feel of the plastic seats on the Parachute Jump at Coney Island. The illusion was so real that I could imagine the whoosh and pop of the nylon canopy exploding open above my head as I plunged downward on a warm day. My fingers can still feel the softness of the lacy silks in the lingerie workrooms in the Garment District. I can remember the glossiness of the costumes on the dancing Rockettes at Radio City Music Hall. They were skirted with graceful netting and spangled with sequins. I remember the tragicomic scene of one stormy, wet night when, emerging from a theater into Times Square, I ran to catch a taxi, slipped instead, and slid beneath a peanut stand wearing the most expensive dress I had ever owned—set off by a perky straw hat. Even to this day, I can remember the feel of that soggy blue silk dress and that cockeyed, broken hat.

As I tried sorting my thoughts one day, I wrestled with the challenge of how to re-create these sorts of fond remembrances in a quilt. It seemed impossible, but then "Ah, ha!" thought I. "If I cannot reconstruct those misty, old tactile sensations, I can fabricate new ones."

My most important memories of New York were of the people—thousands of them everywhere—old, young, all colors, and all cultures. When you stand and look upward in the city, you see miles and miles of windows, and each of those windows has a person behind it. The patterns of these people are interwoven into the fabric of my mind. I decided that if I were to make a quilt about the feeling of New York, it would have to be about the people.

I began to save fabrics for my quilt about this special place. At each fabric store, big or little, I sorted through stacks of flat folds and shelves of bolts looking for cloth with small shapes, things I might find in the rooms behind all those windows. I eventually built a stash that was right for the project. I had prints of flowers, people, furniture, and one with words on it. I found a piece of fabric with an upright hand with a heart in its palm, just right to make a sign for a gypsy tearoom. Another scrap showed women sitting around a quilt frame—an excellent picture for a window! To match this, I found a quilt shop sign for the window of a street-level shop below. Another fabric was printed with chairs. I cut them out and carefully placed them into another window to make a perfect place for elderly men to sit and watch the world outside. I built a window for the couple who would live in a loft in one of my buildings. I hung a flag in their window and put an apple core on the sill. I made a bakery window with lovely, plump pies set out to cool.

My quilt windows were like the windows along the streets of New York. Bit by bit I built a city neighborhood, a fabric neighborhood. As I stitched, I revisited my memories.

Now my quilt is finished, and my street is peopled. Behind all those windows where the people are is a softness quilted into the depth, and I can touch it.

- - - - -

Love's Old Sweet Song

My old, Victorian pump organ stands in my workroom. Sometimes the snibbles of thread cling to it. Sometimes fabric is piled on the keys. Sometimes the dust lies thick in its crevasses and convoluted scrolls. But always, that organ sings to me.

It's a lovely organ with red fabric peeking out between the cut-wood lattice across the music-book ledge. There is a lovely gilt carving of the organ maker centered there. Below it his name is painted in gilt curlicues. The pedals are carpeted and the wood is deep and dark and warm when it is polished.

My organ sits in my workroom, keeping me company in all my moods. Its scrolls and gimcracks hold all my secrets. On days when my spirits are high, I take time to pump out old gospel songs. I especially love the dramatic one called "Do Not Disappoint Your Mother." When I play that one, any of my children who happen to be home go into the other room and ignore me. On quiet, dim, romantic days, I like waltzes. Stephen Foster melodies are fine for gloomy days. If I pull out the "flute" stop, the music is soaring and dramatic. I am a terrible organist, but I sing along. I am a terrible singer, but I love my organ.

Perhaps I love my organ because I am a quilter. I am in love with the softness of the glowing wood, the gentleness of the sound. Its history touches me. I am told that it was made in Coming, New York, in 1874, and it was purchased for a bride. I think this must be true. It is an organ a young bride would have loved.

I am a romantic, you see, and because I am a romantic, I love quilts. Quilts feel soft and gentle. They are warm and comforting. That is why we call them comforters. If we look at quilts, we can imagine all sorts of things about their makers. The best quilt stories have been handed down with them, stories of hardship, endurance, love, sacrifice.

I think that all quilters have that soft spot somewhere. The romantic streak must be genetic, inherited. I met a woman at a quilt meeting yesterday. She is a dentist. I cannot imagine a more practical, technical skill than adjusting and repairing people's teeth, yet she waxed lyrical about her quilts. I meet people of all ilk, some down-to-earth data-processing types, a few very gutsy folk, some gentle and soft-spoken, and they all seem to carry that romantic gene. Sometimes the quality is worn like a flower on the quilter's shoulder. Sometimes it's buried so deep that it is astonishing when we glimpse it. But tell anyone a good quilt story, anyone at all, and you touch that person.

I sit at my organ in the early evening hours while I wait for my microwave to beep, waiting to put supper on the table. I play "Just a Song at Twilight." I sing it. I pull out all the stops and sing it again, loudly and dramatically. Then, I eat my supper and settle in the living room to work on my quilt. As I work on it, I am stitching into it the theme of my daily life. I am creating a little quilt romance of my own.

Declaration of Independence

Driving in the light of dawn, I watched the edges of the road for deer that might dart in front of my car. Instead, a fluttering of wings caught my eye, and I saw an enormous bird, dipping and dancing as it rode the air currents above the pines and birches. Suddenly, the mighty eagle dove and soared beside me, and I held my breath as our eyes met. All that power—all that freedom!

That moment of awe stayed with me as I arrived at the quilt show. The quilt display was enormous; row after row filled with color, imagination, and skill. Each multipieced quilt was a wonder, a triumph in perfection and endurance. Composed of complex compass points, Flying Geese, or marvelous tiny squares with corners meeting perfectly, these quilts symbolized achievement and pride. Some appeared to have a hidden light, glowing from within, while some simply danced. As I wandered from quilt to quilt, I recognized another element in many. The most remarkable quilts were like none I had ever seen.

These quilts happened inside the maker's head, born of his or her inspiration, created with the need to explore, try new things, and take risks. To make quilts like these, we need to flex our wings, gather our courage, and take that long, soaring first solo flight. We need to

- - - - -

fly away from classes and kits and magazine pictures, away from the ideas other people teach us, and into uncharted territory. As we declare our independence and experiment, we learn new techniques and discover what our hands and brains do best. More importantly, we learn what makes us happiest.

Creativity is something each of us carries, a spark deep inside. My personal theory is that the best creation is the result of an error. Each mistake forces us to step out of our planned path and dig deep to creatively cope with the new challenge and to make something beautiful out of the blunder. Quilters are not alone in the art of creative repair. Look at art books, and you'll see the sketches famous artists drew to begin their work; however, you may also see the x-ray pictures of their paintings that show erasures, overpainting, new elements, or changed positions. Whenever I make a mistake, I despair, and then, I repair. Creative embellishments, such as applique and embroidery, are my trusted companions, turning my fault into a triumph.

Making a truly wonderful quilt, one that is all our own and made from the heart, causes us to worry. Will other people like it or not? How will friends, family, and most of all, quilt-show judges view my effort? What opinions will they express? When the comments on the judging slips are good, I love it; if the comments are not, I am sad. Having a judge love your quilt is very nice, but I remind myself that the main reason I quilt is because of the enormous satisfaction I gain from discovering new possibilities. I delight in handling fabrics, stitching, and playing with my ideas. The joy of quiltmaking comes first from experimenting, and then from the surprising results.

All of the quilts at the show were masterpieces, crafted with love, talent, and enormous investments of time. Every one of the quilts flew high, but some flew just a bit higher than those surrounding them. Nestled into each display were these unique quilts, the ones on which the quiltmaker tried something unexpected, original, or perhaps even daring. Doing something different requires curiosity, faith in ourselves, and above all, courage. While learning, we flutter like little birds, finding our strengths and talents, but when at last we declare our independence, we soar like an eagle.

Pretty Contemporary

I am quite happy being an old-fashioned girl, but a touch of contemporary self-improvement is certainly welcome. I've already put my beloved old Featherweight high up on the shelf and replaced it with a dandy computerized sewing machine that does everything but sing and dance. I have set my giant cutting mat out on a big table by the window so that it is always available. My workroom is bright, lit with an array of lamps so that every corner is illuminated. My computer sits right beside my ironing board, and my TV has a place on top of my fabric cupboard. That's being pretty contemporary, I think. Now, I'm even modernizing my quilts.

Alright, I admit that I use 100 percent cotton fabrics, which is old-fashioned. I have tried alternatives, such as artificial fibers and varying weights and weaves of material. I have found that cotton fabrics are easier to piece. Sometimes old ways are better; sometimes new ways are good too.

When I make my quilts, I always begin with old-time quilt blocks. Every one of my quilts has sprung from historical roots, but as I work on them, they morph into variations, changing and adapting so that each project becomes relevant to today's climate.

I've been working on a very large bed quilt. All sorts of shapes and traditional block patterns played through my head. I found a time-honored pattern that satisfied me, and I went off to the quilt shop to find inspiration. I looked at all the fabrics because my plan was to make a large contemporary quilt for a large contemporary bed. Since this would be a fresh, new quilt, I would select modem, stylish materials. After studying this year's color trends, I prowled through exotic Japanese flowers and Persian inspired paisleys. Antique reproductions appealed to me, but in the end, I settled for a brightly colored, swirly print, which seemed a reasonable compromise. This fabric isn't wildly contemporary, but it does have lots of movement and imagination. Choosing bright swirls is certainly an update to my traditional mode.

While I absorbed the excitement and enthusiasm that brews in a quilt shop, I studied the stencils designed for hand quilters. Hand quilting has always been my joy. I love the motion and the tradition of it, but the traditional me gave way to reason. This quilt would be enormous, and I knew that I could not possibly hand quilt it in my lifetime. Instead, I will take my top to an updated, modern woman and have her machine quilt it.

It looks like my traditional quilt has been reshaped to fit this modem world. When I put the last stitch in the binding, it will have mutated, shifted, adapted, and been transformed. It will be new and improved. New dyes, new images, and new inspirations have lured me out of my traditional comfort zone. I am still an old-fashioned girl at heart, but even I am succumbing to the charm of new visions, new ways, and new quilts. That's being pretty contemporary, don't you think?

About the Author

Helen Kelley is a quiltmaker, instructor, lecturer, and author based in Minneapolis, Minnesota. Since she bought her first sewing machine—a Singer Featherweight—in 1946, she has made well over one hundred quilts and wall hangings, many of which are of masterpiece quality and have been displayed at shows both nationally and internationally.

Widely respected by the quilting community, Helen was the first president of the Minnesota Quilter's Guild and has received an abundance of awards for her quilts. In 1999, at the International Quilt Festival in Houston, Texas, her "Renaissance Quilt" was chosen as one of the 100 Best American Quilts of the Twentieth Century.

Helen's "Loose Threads" articles have appeared monthly in *Quilters Newsletter* for twenty-five years. Written in wry and pertinent language, the column has long been a favorite of readers. Her previous books include *Every Quilt Tells a Story, Helen Kelley's Joy of Quilting, Scarlet Ribbons: American Indian Technique for Today's Quilters,* and *Dating Quilts.* She was also featured in Oxmoor House's *Quilt with the Best.* In addition, Helen's byline has appeared in a variety of quilting publications, and her prize-winning quilts have been the subject of numerous photo essays.

Helen is the 2008 inductee into the prestigious Quilters Hall of Fame.